Col E.

D0149542

WITHDRAWN
UTSA LIBRARIES

RUSSIAN
VERSIFICATION

Oxford University Press, Ely House, London W. 1

GLASGOW NEW YORK TORONTO MELBOURNE WELLINGTON
CAPE TOWN SALISBURY IBADAN NAIROBI LUSAKA ADDIS ABABA
BOMBAY CALCUTTA MADRAS KARACHI LAHORE DACCA
KUALA LUMPUR HONG KONG

RUSSIAN VERSIFICATION

BY

B. O. UNBEGAUN

PROFESSOR OF COMPARATIVE SLAVONIC PHILOLOGY
IN THE UNIVERSITY OF OXFORD
AND FELLOW OF BRASENOSE COLLEGE

OXFORD
AT THE CLARENDON PRESS

Free verse is like free love;
it is a contradiction in terms.

G. K. CHESTERTON

FIRST PUBLISHED 1956
REPRINTED PHOTOGRAPHICALLY FROM CORRECTED SHEETS
OF THE FIRST EDITION 1963, 1966

PRINTED IN GREAT BRITAIN
AT THE UNIVERSITY PRESS, OXFORD
BY VIVIAN RIDLER, PRINTER TO THE UNIVERSITY

LIBRARY
The University of Texas
At San Antonio

PREFACE

THERE is no account of Russian versification available to the ordinary non-Russian reader, and those written in Russian, though certainly very useful, tend to be obscured by detail and do not, on the whole, give a clear idea of the subject. Also, these studies contradict one another, sometimes over essential questions of Russian prosody. The omission, therefore, encourages me to offer this study, in which I have revised and combined a course that I gave in 1942 at the University of Strasbourg, transferred at that time to Clermont-Ferrand, with a series of lectures at Oxford in October 1950.

My purpose is to describe the structure of Russian verse by establishing its fundamental principles and separating them from the mass of secondary detail. Consequently this study is limited to the purely technical aspect of Russian versification, and excludes general information on poetic language and style, and all discussion of tropes, figures of speech, order of words, their choice and their value, and so forth.

It follows also that my chief concern is with the versification of the last hundred and fifty years, that is to say from the time of Zhukovsky onwards. Russian verse of the seventeenth and eighteenth centuries is examined here with the sole aim of explaining the development of modern verse.

As is fitting, the text abounds in illustrations from poetical works. Needless to say, these passages are quoted not for their aesthetic value, but for the exclusively technical interest their versification affords. Yet, as far as possible, I have been careful to avoid drawing upon second-rate poets, though, clearly, such discrimination is influenced by my own likes and dislikes.

A passage illustrating a particular feature of versification—enjambment for example—can usually serve to illustrate other verse elements too, such as the metrical structure, the caesura and rhyme. Thus frequent cross-references are needed. As every example carries metrical stresses, it will not come as a surprise to find the stress on a monosyllable.

For the convenience of the reader, I have been careful to point out the metrical structure of each passage quoted, even when this aspect has no bearing on the matter under consideration.

Alongside the English terms the Russian equivalents are given. Curiously enough, in matters of prosody, Russian terminology seems to be more standardized than English. The best I could do was to choose from the mass of English terms, often confused and contradictory, those which in my opinion best suited Russian verse.

B. O. U.

Oxford
March 1955

CONTENTS

INTRODUCTION

THE language of poetry is far from spontaneous. On the contrary, it is highly artificial: nobody employs verse in ordinary speech. Therefore, the rules governing prosody must also be conventional. In Russian prosody these rules have changed with time. That is why this study, while dealing essentially with modern versification, necessarily includes frequent historical references.

The first Russian verse of any importance made its appearance fairly late—one might even say very late—in the second half of the seventeenth century. Consequently, the history of Russian versification is contained in less than three hundred years. Within this short period only the last two hundred years represent what could be described as modern poetry. The previous century is dominated by conceptions of poetry different from those prevailing today. It is a common view in Russia that there is no link between these two conceptions, but this impression is a superficial one. Indeed, there is no break in the evolution of Russian prosody, any more than there is in that of Russian civilization. One of my tasks will be to show the continuity of Russian versification.

Modern Russian versification has several points in common with that of other European literatures, in particular German and English. The explanation of this is partly that the Russians borrowed several rules of prosody from western Europe, and partly that throughout the world there are not many such rules from which to choose.

What are the fundamental principles of versification, those which distinguish the language of poetry from the language of prose?

Versification is based on the principle of a regular alternation of strong and weak syllables. This principle can be applied to most systems of verse-writing, but the actual notion of what constitutes a strong syllable varies according to the language.

Normally, for marking the strong syllable language uses its most salient feature, which is either the quantity, i.e. length, of the syllable, or its stress. Thus, in European languages there are roughly two main types of versification, of which one is based on the alternation of long and short syllables, and the other depends on the alternation of stressed and unstressed syllables.

The Greeks used a versification based on quantity, although their language also possessed word-stress. This stress, however, was subordinate to quantity and was not free. Greek prosody was closely connected with song, for Greek verse was composed in order to be sung. This explains, to some extent at least, why classical verse, considered apart from its musical nature, either sounds artificial to our ears or else evokes no response at all. The metrical unit of Greek verse, the *foot*, is composed of two or more syllables, long or short. Based on the idea of duration, the foot corresponds to a musical bar. Stress does not appear at all in classical prosody.

The Greek prosody was adopted in Latin verse, although it appears that native Italic poetry was based on stress. The so-called Saturnian verse may be regarded as a survival of the latter.

At the beginning of the Middle Ages, however, Latin poetry abandoned the imported quantitative principle. The early medieval Latin verse, preserved mainly in the form of hymns, was reduced to a set number of syllables in the line, with an occasional regular distribution of stresses. This medieval prosody was inherited by almost all European literatures. But each of them adapted this prosody to the possibilities offered by its own national language.

At first, medieval Latin verse was adopted by Romance languages. It is easy to understand how the modern French prosody has grown out of the Latin. The word-stress was too weak in French to give form to the verse, and the only remnant of the medieval Latin prosody which was retained by French poetry was a set number of syllables in the line. Obviously, that alone could not give character to a line of verse, and it was here that stress made its appearance, though discreetly, as a subordinate element in the language should, in order to mark the end of the line and the end of the hemistich. Moreover, such verse-writing takes into consideration accentual groups within the line.

This type of verse is normally used by Romance languages. In Italian, however, stress, which plays a more important role than in French, plays a more significant part in the verse structure as well. The same verse was adopted also in Polish, naturally enough, since in Polish the accent always falls on the same syllable (the last but one), and for that reason it is weak and has no semantic value. This type of verse, based on the sole constant principle of a given number of syllables in each line, may be called *syllabic verse* (in Russian: силлабический стих).

In the Germanic languages—English and German— medieval Latin versification has developed differently, through coming into contact with native popular verse, which was based solely upon stress. This popular verse was characterized by a set number of stresses in each line, regardless of its total number of syllables, though the number of syllables between the stresses varied. Subordinate elements could reinforce the pattern, and of these the most usual, in Old English and Old German poetry, was alliteration. This type of versification entered learned poetry too. One finds it in poets like Heine (as for example in *Die Lorelei*) or Coleridge (as for example in *Christabel*). This verse of irregularly distributed stress may be called *accentual verse* (in Russian: тонический стих).

It is especially common in modern English and German poetry to find the features of accentual native verse applied to the imported syllabic versification. This type of verse combined in each line a given number of stresses with a given number of syllables whose stresses are distributed regularly throughout the line. This verse, as combining the principles of both the syllabic and the accentual verse, may be termed *syllabic-accentual verse* (in Russian: силлábo-тонический стих).

Russian poetry used and still uses all the three types of verse described above. Syllabic verse was imported from Poland in the middle of the seventeenth century, but disappeared a hundred years later. The German type of syllabic-accentual verse was introduced into Russia towards the middle of the eighteenth century—a natural process when one remembers that in Russian, as in English and German, stress plays an important part, and must necessarily be equally significant in versification. The Russian tradition, however, differs somewhat from the English and German. These differences will be discussed later. The purely accentual verse had in Russian poetry a less uniform origin. But clearly its links with the native popular verse are weak.

To sum up then, in most European languages, the modern versification is imported. And it seems that, originating abroad in this way, learned poetry acquires a prestige which popular native songs and poems cannot confer upon it. There is no reason to oppose so natural a development. In any case, it is unreasonable to accept the view often stated in textbooks on literature, that such and such a prosody of foreign origin should be rejected on the ground that it violates native usage. Certainly it does. But every type of versification does that for the simple reason that no one uses verse in ordinary speech. The important thing is to make sure that the prosody chosen does not harm it too obviously.

Besides the learned poetry with which this study deals, the Russians have made folk-poetry, consisting of epic poems and songs, ever since the Middle Ages. This folk-poetry remained unwritten until in the eighteenth century a number of lovers of folk-lore took it into their heads to write down some specimens of it. It was meant to be sung and its rhythmic structure, based upon accentual groups, can really be understood only by reference to its musical function. Russian literary verse does not come from folk-poetry. It has never done more than use from time to time certain examples of popular verse, in order to imitate particular rhythmical devices contained in it. Folk-poetry will be referred to in this study only because of these imitations; it will not be examined systematically.

I

SYLLABIC VERSE

EVER since the twelfth century, which marked the beginning of their literary experience, the Russians seem to have been familiar with examples of learned poetry, imported from the Balkans. These were written in Old Church Slavonic—the name given to the Macedonian dialect into which Saints Cyril and Methodius translated the Scriptures and liturgical books. This type of poetry was no more than a simple adaptation of Greek literary verse of the Byzantine era, and the only principle governing this early Slavonic versification seems to have been a fixed number of syllables in the line. This imported poetry disappeared very soon, and Russian literature contained no learned poetry throughout the Middle Ages.

Poetry did not appear again in Russian literature until the beginning of the seventeenth century. At first it was quite primitive poetry. The only feature which distinguished it from prose was the rhyme, which was always in couplets. Neither the number of syllables, nor, still less, the distribution of stress was taken into account. The use of rhyme was not unknown in Russia during the Middle Ages: sayings and proverbs were frequently in rhyme or assonance. But the application of rhyme to whole poems at the beginning of the seventeenth century seems to have been due originally to the imitation of the form of Ukrainian poetry, which consisted of rhymed imparisyllabic lines. Here, for example, is an extract from a poem by Ivan

B

Nasedka, written about 1625, in which the author expresses his indignation at the sight of the Lutheran church in the castle of Frederiksborg in Denmark, which he had visited in 1621:

Въ толи́ку убо го́рдость коро́ль онъ, Христіа́нусъ, произыде́,
Я́ко же и сатана́ на се́верныя го́ры мы́слію изыде́:
Горѣ́ убо устро́ивъ двоекро́вную пола́ту,
До́лу же подъ не́ю двоеимя́нную ропа́ту,
И по-лю́терски нарица́ютъ ихъ двѣ́ ки́рки,
По-ру́сски же ви́димъ ихъ: отво́рены лю́торемъ во а́дъ двѣ ди́рки.
Горѣ́ убо устро́енъ въ пола́тѣ блу́да и пія́нства сто́лъ,
До́лу же подъ ни́мъ приноше́нія спасе́нія ихъ на Бо́жій престо́лъ.
Мно́гихъ же вво́дятъ въ ки́рку ту смы́слу короле́вску диви́тися,
Велеу́мнымъ же муже́мъ не подоба́етъ безу́мію ихъ диви́тися.

This type of poetry existed throughout the seventeenth century, even after the appearance of syllabic poetry. Here, as a further example, is the opening of a love letter, dated 1698, which has been preserved only because it was used as evidence in a case of theft:

Оче́й мои́хъ пресла́вну свѣ́ту
И не ле́стному на́шему совѣ́ту.
Здра́ва бу́ди, душа́ моя, мно́гія лѣ́та
И не забыва́й пра́веднаго твоего́ обѣ́та,
Какъ мы съ тобо́й передъ Бо́гомъ обѣща́лися,
Въ кото́рое вре́мя пе́рстнями помѣня́лися
И вѣнцы́ наши на глава́хъ нашихъ имѣ́ли златы́е,
Во дни́ мимоше́дшіе ра́достные, святы́е,
Поча́сту, свѣ́те моя, вспомина́й,
Наипа́че же въ моли́твахъ свои́хъ не забыва́й.

It may be seen that, in this type of poetry, rhyme can be masculine, feminine, or dactylic.[1]

Owing to one great advantage, though, this primitive poetry did not perish as a result of the final triumph of syllabic-accentual verse: the simplicity of its technique

---

[1] For a definition of these terms, see p. 133.

made it possible for anybody to write it. Therefore, when it disappeared from the surface of literature, it descended to the inferior social classes as a kind of poetry not meant to be sung, in contrast to the poetry which was sung. There it became mingled up with the rhyming methods of Russian proverbs and sayings, almost all of which were rhymed in the seventeenth century, and with popular stories containing occasional rhymes.[1]

II. SYLLABIC VERSE

Real syllabic poetry made its appearance in Russia only towards the middle of the seventeenth century. Three features distinguished it from the primitive poetry which has just been examined: (*a*) the fixed number of syllables in each line, (*b*) the presence of a caesura, i.e. a break in the line,[2] and (*c*) the exclusively feminine rhyme. But there was still no distribution of accent in this kind of poetry. It displayed every feature of Polish poetry, and indeed it was from Poland, via the Ukraine, that syllabic verse came to Russia. As in every language with fixed stress—in Polish the stress is on the penultimate syllable—the word-accent in Polish was too weak to provide a basis for versification. So it is quite natural that at first Polish should make use of the syllabic verse. Later, mainly in the nineteenth century, Polish tried to adopt the syllabic-accentual verse.

The syllabic verse was by its nature much less suited to Russian. Yet it must be said that its application did not involve too serious a violation of the Russian language. Its defect was that it did not exploit the accentual possibilities with which Russian could invest prosody. Unfortunately also for Russian poetry, Polish syllabic verse, after flourishing

---

[1] See p. 108.   Concerning the caesura, see p. 59.

in the sixteenth century, underwent an obvious decline in the seventeenth century, and it was this degenerate verse which the Russians copied. Polish poetry was destined to revive only in the eighteenth century.

Adapted to Russian, the syllabic verse could but result in an artificial reading of poems: the word-accent was unnaturally weakened, and the lines were read, syllable by syllable, with a monotonous cadence. That this style of reading did not shock Russians too much is due largely to the fact that at first syllabic poetry was written not in Russian but in Church Slavonic showing only traces of Russian influence.

Syllabic poetry could not expect to survive long in Russia. It coincided with the influence exercised by Polish–Ukrainian culture, that is to say with the seventeenth century, and fell into desuetude about 1740.

The syllabic poetry attained at once a certain standard with the monk Simeon Polotsky (1629–80), the first poet to appear at the Russian Court, who was tutor to the Tsar's children, and a White Russian by origin. He is a genuine example of the baroque in Russian poetry. Unfortunately, his work, consisting of some fifty thousand lines, has remained largely unpublished. Here are quotations from his poetry, in which the caesura is indicated by the two vertical dashes:

> Хамелео́нту вражда́ ‖ естество́мъ всади́ся
>   къ живо́тнымъ, ихъ же жало ‖ я́да испо́лнися.
> Ви́дя у́бо онъ змі́я, ‖ на дре́во всхожда́етъ
>   и изъ устъ нить на него́ ‖ нѣ́кую пуща́етъ;
> Въ ея́ же концѣ́ ка́пля, ‖ что би́серъ, сия́етъ,
>   ю́же онъ ного́ю на ‖ змі́я управля́етъ.
> Та повнегда́ змі́евѣй ‖ главѣ́ прикосне́тся,
>   а́бие ядоно́сный ‖ умерщвле́нъ простре́тся.[1]

---

[1] Труды отдела древне-русской литературы, VI (1948), p. 131.

Полудень

О́же среде́ небесе́ ‖ со́лнце бѣгъ свой дѣетъ,
   па́литъ ни́вы, а скоты́ ‖ лучми́ зѣло́ грѣетъ,
И́же въ сѣни́ при вода́хъ ‖ отъ трудо́въ кладя́тся, —
   жнеци́ пи́щею и сно́мъ ‖ по трудѣхъ крѣпя́тся.
Такъ ество́ о́тчески ‖ стро́итъ е́же бы́ти:
   зако́нъ всѣмъ пи́шетъ вещѐмъ ‖ ну́ждный сохрапи́ти.[1]

Like most of Simeon Polotsky's poems, these two extracts are in lines of thirteen syllables—the Polish equivalent of the Alexandrine—with the caesura after the
seventh syllable, despite the sense in line six of the first
extract: на ‖ змия. In theory the distribution of stress has
no importance in this versification, except in the example
of the compulsory stress on the twelfth syllable. However,
it will be noticed that in the second extract an obvious
attempt has been made to bring in a fairly regular rhythmic cadence, which calls to mind the trochaic line.[2]

Here is a description of America written at the end of
the seventeenth century by another poet, Karion Istomin,
who was born shortly before 1650, and died in 1717. It
occurs in the work *Polis*, a kind of huge rhymed ency-
clopaedia:

Аме́рика ‖ ча́сть четве́рта,
Но́во земля́ ‖ взна́нь отпе́рта.
Волнохи́щна ‖ Аме́рика
Людми́ въ нра́вахъ ‖ въ ца́рствахъ ди́ка.
Ты́сящми лѣтъ ‖ бысть пе зна́нна,
Мо́ремъ зѣло́ ‖ отлі́яна,
Вѣры ра́зны ‖ въ балвохва́лствѣ,
На́ги лю́ди ‖ тамъ въ недба́лствѣ.
Ца́рства иму́тъ ‖ безъ ра́зума:
Не зна́въ Бо́га, ‖ худа́ ду́ма.
Никто́ же бо ‖ что успѣетъ,
Гдѣ глу́пость скве́рнь ‖ и грѣхъ дѣетъ.

[1] Ibid., p. 135.   [2] See p. 6.

The poem is written in lines of eight syllables, divided by the caesura into two equal parts.

One of the important features of seventeenth-century poetry is that it is written in Church Slavonic. In its Russian variant, syllabic poetry found a master in Antiochus Kantemir (1708–44), of whose poetry an example follows, in lines of thirteen syllables:

Огонь и восковой болван

Иску́сный в де́ле свое́м ‖ восколе́й, приле́жно
Труди́вся, изли́л болва́н, ‖ все вы́разив не́жно
В нем у́ды, ча́сти, власы́ ‖ так что жи́во те́ло
Болва́нчика того́ бы́ть ‖ вся́к бы сказа́л сме́ло.
Око́нчив всё, не умно́ ‖ забы́л отдали́ти
Болва́н от огня́, где во́ск ‖ случи́лось топи́ти.
Ося́гл жа́р пла́мени во́ск, ‖ расползло́ся те́ло
Болва́нчика; пропа́л тру́д, ‖ пропа́ло все де́ло.
Кто де́ло свое́ верши́в, ‖ утверди́ть жела́ет
В до́лги ве́ки, до́лжен всё, ‖ что тому́ меша́ет,
Отдаля́ть, и что вреди́т ‖ — искореня́ть ско́ро;
Без того́ де́ло его́ ‖ не мо́жет быть спо́ро.

(1731)

The same principles still apply, but the verse has certainly increased in suppleness. There are two reasons for this. First, the caesura became more uniform, being placed regularly after a stressed syllable, as, for example, in the last extract quoted.[1] The second reason is the more important. This was Kantemir's attempt to introduce a more regular cadence into the verse, in other words to place the stress at more or less regular intervals, thus making use of the natural advantages that Russian affords in poetry. Polish syllabic verse, made up of words whose accents fall on the penultimate syllable, inclined to the trochaic rhythm. Kantemir, in trying to introduce a pattern of more regular rhythm in syllabic verse, finished, as could have been

---

[1] For further details and examples, see pp. 59–60, 138–9.

expected, by emphasizing still further its trochaic cadence. From this stage it was but a short step to a pure trochaic line, excluding the stress from even syllables. This step was taken within Kantemir's lifetime by his contemporary, Vasily Trediakovsky.

Syllabic poetry, in spite of its disappearance around 1740, still had some influence on Russian versification in the ensuing period; and, in the eighteenth and early nineteenth centuries, in addition to the choice of rhyme, it accounts for the way in which verse was recited, and the preponderance of binary metres.

II

SYLLABIC-ACCENTUAL VERSE: METRICAL STRUCTURE

I. GENERAL PRINCIPLES

To Vasily Trediakovsky (1703–69), as it is generally admitted, is due the credit for having first discerned the principles of modern versification. In common with the other poets, he began by writing syllabic poetry, but soon realized that this type of versification did not take into account that essential feature of the Russian language, the word-stress. This he made the foundation of the new versification in a treatise which appeared in 1735: Новый и краткій способъ къ сложенію россійскихъ стіховъ. Nevertheless he still remained partially enslaved by the syllabic tradition. For, though recognizing the foot made up of one stressed and one unstressed syllable, i.e. the trochee ($\perp$ –) or the iambus (– $\perp$), as the unit of Russian verse, he recommended only the use of the trochee, and the iambus, in his opinion, was to be avoided. Evidently for him the iambus caused, so to speak, a mere breach in trochaic verse, a breach that he was prepared to allow, though with some regret; and it is typical that, as an example of the new type of versification, he quoted from Kantemir a line of which the trochaic cadence was far from pure:

Умъ толь слабый плодъ трудовъ краткія науки.

Also Trediakovsky considered only what he called 'heroic verse', that is to say a traditional line of thirteen syllables;

he did not admit trisyllabic feet, which is additional evidence of the bondage he suffered from the syllabic verse.

In 1752, Trediakovsky published a new edition of his treatise: Способъ къ сложенію россійскихъ стиховъ противъ выданнаго въ 1735 годѣ исправленный и дополненный. There is little in common between the two editions. In the second, Trediakovsky admitted the iambus on an equal footing with the trochee, and there was no longer any question of tolerating, as he did with some reluctance in 1735, the mixture, in the same line, of iambuses and trochees. Even trisyllabic feet were permitted. In short, this was a faithful enough picture of modern Russian versification, whose success, however, was due less to this theoretical treatise and to the early practical experiments of Trediakovsky than to the brilliant poetical writings of his contemporary Michael Lomonosov (1711–65). One may even wonder if the second treatise would have received its final shape without the convincing example set by Lomonosov's verse.

As a guide to his theory of poetry, Lomonosov has left nothing but a letter addressed to the Academy of Sciences in 1739: Письмо о правилахъ россійскаго стихотворства, in which he appealed to the only sound principle: namely, that versification should be adapted to the natural resources of Russian and should borrow nothing inconsistent with them. He declared himself in favour of binary as well as ternary metres. But he also accepted in the structure of the verse alongside iambuses, trochees, anapaests, and dactyls—he is ignorant of amphibrachs—a free mixture of iambuses and anapaests as well as of trochees and dactyls, an ultimate tribute to the classical tradition.[1]

What this change in versification meant to Russian

---

[1] The mixture of iambuses and anapaests he gave as an example is quoted on page 101.

poetry is vividly exemplified by an ode of Trediakovsky.
The ode, composed on the occasion of the coronation of
the Empress Anna, was written in 1730, and followed the
syllabic versification. These are the opening lines:

> Да здра́вствует днесь Импера́трикс А́нна
> На престо́л се́дша увенча́нна,
> Красне́йша Со́лнца и звезд сия́юща ны́не!
> Да здра́вствует на мно́га ле́та,
> Пофи́рою злато́й оде́та
> В импера́торском чи́не.

In the 1752 edition of Trediakovsky's works, the same ode
appeared, rewritten according to the new theory of versification, in free iambic lines. The difference is striking:

> Да здра́вствует вовек Императри́ца А́нна,
> Восше́дша на престо́л уже́ и увенча́нна,
> Красне́йше всех свети́л
> Сия́ющая ны́не!
> В свое́й ту благосты́не
> Бог свы́ше оцени́л.

The syllabic verse had been borrowed from Poland.
Syllabic-accentual poetry, according to Trediakovsky, had
followed the practice of popular Russian poetry. However,
that was true only in so far as the pioneers of the new versification had recognized in the word-stress the very basis of
the rhythm. The stresses, though, are distributed at regular
intervals, so that, except in some few trochaic metres, the
real basis of syllabic-accentual verse, especially in the
iambic line, seems to have been the result of the application
in Russian of German prosody. It is significant that the
first syllabic-accentual poetry in Russian was written long
before that of Trediakovsky and Lomonosov by foreigners
who knew Russian, namely by Germans and Swedes.[1] They

---

[1] See V. N. Peretts, Историко-литературныя изслѣдованія и
матеріалы. Томъ III. Изъ исторіи развитія русской поэзіи XVIII в.,
часть 1–2, Спб., 1902 (Записки Историко-филологическаго факуль-

were not bound by any syllabic tradition, and a great part of their work consisted in translations of German poems, especially church-hymns. The poems composed by two Germans from Saxony, the Pastor Johann Ernst Glück (1652–1705) and Johann Werner Paus (1670–1734), were particularly remarkable. Their poetry has never been published and, therefore, could not have considerably influenced Russian prosody. It can hardly be believed, however, that Trediakovsky and Lomonosov took no account of it. As this poetry is very little known, some specimens of it are included in the present study.[1]

The syllabic-accentual verse, which has dominated Russian poetry for two hundred years, is based on the regular alternation of stressed (strong) and unstressed (weak) syllables. Clearly it is, in the main, the type of German and English versification.

The unit of Russian syllabic-accentual verse is the line (стих). To characterize the different metres of the line, the conventional concept of foot (стопá) is used. To describe the foot, which can comprise either two or three syllables, a terminology is used in Russian which originates from ancient versification, and even its graphic symbols – and ◡, are often borrowed. Both terminology and symbols were introduced by Trediakovsky in 1735. But these imported terms are used to express entirely different ideas: in the metrical scheme borrowed from the Greek prosody, Russian substitutes the stressed for the long syllable and the unstressed for the short. A *Greek iambus* is a foot of two syllables, the first being short and the second long: ◡ –. A *Russian iambus* is also disyllabic, but the first syllable is unstressed

тета Имп. Санктпетербургскаго Университета, lxiv). P. N. Berkov, 'Из истории русской поэзии первой трети XVIII века', in XVIII век: сборник статей и материалов (Ленинград, 1935), pp. 61–81.

[1] See pp. 22, 25, 28, 49.

and the second stressed: $- \acute{-}$.[1] A *Greek dactyl* is a foot of three syllables in which the first is long and the remaining two short: $- \cup \cup$. A *Russian dactyl* combines a stressed syllable with two unstressed syllables following it: $\acute{-} - -$. Similarly the structure of all other feet may be calculated.

There is no notion of duration in Russian versification beyond the fact that the stressed syllable is always longer than the unstressed; but this fact affects the prosody no more than it does the spoken language, with the result that a Russian is not even conscious of it.

Each line in the Russian syllabic-accentual verse is said then to be composed of a certain number of feet. These comprise one stressed and one or two unstressed syllables. Feet with more than three syllables do not exist in Russian, and any examples in which one might be tempted to assume their existence may be explained by the omission of stress in lines of disyllabic feet, or by the combination of different feet, or yet again by accentual verse. Thus Russian possesses feet of five different varieties:

In binary metre (двухдо́льный разме́р) there are two feet of two syllables:

   1. The iambus (ямб): $- \acute{-}$.
   2. The trochee (хоре́й, less usually трохе́й): $\acute{-} -$.

In ternary metre (трехдо́льный разме́р) there are three feet of three syllables:

   1. The dactyl (да́ктиль): $\acute{-} - -$.
   2. The amphibrach (амфибра́хий): $- \acute{-} -$.
   3. The anapaest (анапе́ст): $- - \acute{-}$.

At this stage it is important to notice three general

---

[1] Henceforward the syllable will be shown by means of a dash and the stress by means of an acute over the top of the dash. This notation, besides avoiding any confusion with Greek and Latin prosody, affords further advantages, as will be seen.

principles governing Russian versification of the syllabic-accentual type.

1. As has already been pointed out, the real unit of Russian syllabic-accentual verse is the line, and the foot is but a conventional, though a very convenient, concept. The foot does not exist independently of the line. Therefore a term such as 'four-foot trochaic line' does not suggest that this line is a result of a sequence of four independent disyllabic units called 'trochees'. It only implies, in a remarkably concise way, that this line may have from seven to nine syllables, that the even syllables are unstressed and the seventh is always stressed, whereas the first, third, and fifth syllables may be stressed or not. It follows from the conventional character of the foot that the metrical breaking-up of a line into feet is independent of the real breaking-up of a sentence into words: they need not coincide one with another.

2. The metrical stresses of the line must not be inconsistent with the natural stress of the word. A change of stress in a word to make it comply with rhythmic demands is not allowed. The few cases in which this requirement is infringed are occasioned either by bad verse or by artificial effect intended by the poet. This will be discussed later.

3. Whatever the metre used, the regular succession of strong and weak syllables concludes with the last stress of the line. The final unstressed syllables following the last stress are completely independent of the metrical structure of the line. Thus line-endings of three different types may occur:

(a) The end of the line may coincide with the end of the last foot; in this case the line is composed of a given number of complete feet.

(b) One, two, very rarely three unstressed syllables may be added to the last foot.

(c) The last foot may be truncated and lacking the last unstressed syllable in a trochaic or amphibrachic line or the last two unstressed syllables in a dactylic line.

All these devices are used to alternate masculine, feminine, or dactylic rhymes and will be examined in Chapter VI, of which the subject is rhyme.

The division of feet will be indicated by a vertical dash.

II. BINARY METRES

Binary metres comprise two variants:

1. The iambic metre, based on the iambic foot $(- \acute{})$.
2. The trochaic metre, based on the trochaic foot $(\acute{} -)$.

1. *The iambic metre*

The iambic line has always been the most commonly used in Russian poetry. Iambic lines, for example, form 84 per cent. of the entire poetic output of Pushkin. Boratynsky, one of the most famous of Pushkin's contemporaries, wrote in all 222 poems, of which 195 are in iambic metre; and this number excludes his longer poems, all of which are in iambics.

Though losing something of its importance in the present century, the iambic still remains the favourite metre of Russian poetry.

In lines written in iambic metre, every even syllable is *strong*, and every odd syllable is *weak*. The strong syllables are in principle stressed, but the weak syllables are unstressed. For example:

Закат сия́л улы́бкой а́лой,	$- \acute{} \mid - \acute{} \mid - \acute{} \mid - \acute{} \mid -$
Пари́ж тону́л в лило́вой мгле́,	$- \acute{} \mid - \acute{} \mid - \acute{} \mid - \acute{}$
В поры́ве гру́сти де́нь уста́лый	$- \acute{} \mid - \acute{} \mid - \acute{} \mid - \acute{} \mid -$
Прижа́л свой ло́б к сыро́й земле́.	$- \acute{} \mid - \acute{} \mid - \acute{} \mid - \acute{}$

М. Волощин, „Пари́ж"

These four lines of four feet each, with their stresses regularly distributed over all the strong syllables, following the metrical scheme adopted, represent the simplest example of iambic verse; the simplest but not the most common.[1] It took a long time to discover in modern poetry this quatrain in which the *metrical scheme* coincides with the *rhythmic pattern*. These terms call for elucidation. By the metrical scheme is meant the specific arrangement of the regular sequence of stressed and unstressed syllables, which is determined by the choice of the measure. The poet must submit to the metrical scheme as it is, but having chosen it, there are various rhythmic possibilities open to him. The individual way in which the poet treats his self-imposed *metre* (метр) or *measure* (размéр) can be called *rhythm* (ритм). This distinction, it appears, considerably facilitates the understanding of Russian syllabic-accentual poetry. In the quatrain quoted, the metre and the rhythm are identical. But, as has been said, this is not the case very frequently. Here is an example of four-foot iambic quatrain, in which the rhythmic pattern diverges from the metrical scheme:

Татья́на то вздохнёт, то о́хнет,	$- \acute{} \mid - \overset{(}{}{} \mid - \acute{} \mid - \acute{} \mid -$
Письмо́ дрожи́т в её руке́,	$- \acute{} \mid - \acute{} \mid - \acute{} \mid - \acute{}$
Обла́тка ро́зовая со́хнет	$- \acute{} \mid - \acute{} \mid - \overset{(}{}{} \mid - \acute{} \mid -$
На воспалённом языке́.	$- \overset{(}{}{} \mid - \acute{} \mid - \overset{(}{}{} \mid - \acute{}$

А. Пу́шкин, „Евге́ний Оне́гин"

By keeping strictly to the metrical scheme with, in each line, the four stresses on the even syllables, the scansion does not correspond with the Russian tradition of recitation, according to which the stresses enclosed in brackets are omitted. Thus, of the four stresses demanded by the metre: the first line omits the second stress (то); the second does not omit any, although the third may be considerably weakened (её); the third line omits the third

[1] For another example, see p. 21.

stress (ро́зовая); and the fourth line omits the first and third stresses (воспалённом and языке́).

The question now arises, under what conditions can strong syllables, i.e. those which are expected to be stressed —in the iambic line the even syllables—remain unstressed? This can happen in the following cases:

1. A Russian word cannot have more than one stress. As a rule, Russian lacks the secondary stress, so frequent in English and German. Thus when a word is spread over more than one foot and besides its normal stress, in accordance with the exigencies of the metre, ought to have a second stress, this second stress does not appear: ро́зова̋я, во̋спалённом, я̋зыке́.

2. Russian possesses a certain number of secondary words, monosyllabic and disyllabic, which are unstressed: they are either enclitic in that they are supported by the word that precedes them, or proclitic in that they are attached in pronunciation to the word which follows them. These are conjunctions, prepositions, and particles. When they occur in a strong position in the line, and require metrical stress, this stress is not applied. In the example given this occurs with the particle то in the first line.

3. In Russian a considerable number of words occur, especially adverbs and various kinds of pronoun, which are normally unstressed, but which in certain circumstances can be given stress. These conditions are generally determined by the meaning. The ambiguous character of the words in question usually results in a partial loss of stress. In the example given this happens to the genitive её in the second line.

What has just been said will become still clearer on examining the following quatrain, which is composed in five-foot iambic lines, and would be described in English terminology as an Elegiac stanza:

О доблестях, о подвигах, о славе $- \acute{-} | -- | - \acute{-} | -- | - \acute{-} | -$
Я забывал на горестной земле, $-- | - \acute{-} | - \acute{-} | -- | - \acute{-}$
Когда твоё лицо в простой оправе $- \acute{-} | -- | - \acute{-} | - \acute{-} | - \acute{-} | -$
Передо мной сияло на столе. $-- | - \acute{-} | - \acute{-} | -- | - \acute{-}$

А. Блок

In this passage the metrical stresses are omitted: (1) on long words, covering more than one foot: доблестя́х, по́двига́х, забыва́л, го́рестно́й; (2) on unstressed words: пере́до, на́; (3) on a word with ambiguous stress: твоё. Here a reading with the stress falling on твоё would be quite in order, in which case когда would lose its stress and the first two feet of the third line would read: $-- | - \acute{-}$.

It will have been seen that, in the examples quoted, the final stress is never left out. This is no chance occurrence. In binary metre the stress on the last foot is obligatory. Any other accent is subject to omission. The choice of accents which may be omitted belongs to the poet and constitutes the rhythmic variation of the given metrical scheme, as has already been mentioned: it is the personal intervention of the poet within the framework he has imposed upon himself. Although in theory his choice may be free, some types of combination occur more frequently than others. Statistics have been compiled on the distribution of stresses, especially regarding the four-foot iambic line, by far the most common metre in Russian verse.

In the *four-foot iambic* line the six following combinations are possible, and are illustrated with examples from Pushkin's poetry:

1. 4 stresses $- \acute{-} | - \acute{-} | - \acute{-} | - \acute{-}$ сердито бился дождь в окно
2. 3 stresses $-- | - \acute{-} | - \acute{-} | - \acute{-}$ на берегу пустынных волн
3.   — $- \acute{-} | -- | - \acute{-} | - \acute{-}$ в Европу прорубить окно
4.   — $- \acute{-} | - \acute{-} | -- | - \acute{-}$ и пунша пламень голубой
5. 2 stresses $-- | - \acute{-} | -- | - \acute{-}$ адмиралтейская игла
6.   — $- \acute{-} | -- | -- | - \acute{-}$ и кланялся непринуждённо

In theory two further combinations may be considered:

7. 2 stresses $- - \mid - - \mid - \underset{\smile}{\prime} \mid - \underset{\smile}{\prime}$ и велосипедист летит
8. 1 stress $- - \mid - - \mid - - \mid - \underset{\smile}{\prime}$ хоть и не без предубежденья

In practice these combinations do not exist and these illustrations are *ad hoc* inventions. When they seem to occur, a weakened stress on the first foot may always be heard.[1]

It goes without saying that a four-foot iambic line, with a single stress, is unimaginable unless the stress falls invariably on the last foot, as in the case of the eighth combination. Any example of a single intermediate stress would automatically call also for a final stress, and so the line would contain two. If the entire line is taken up with a single word, the resulting impression would be strange, not to say ridiculous, and may be exploited for comic effect, as in the following quatrain:[2]

> Брига́да на́ша, отступа́я,
> Распа́лась вся́, исче́зла вся́:
> Неудовлетвори́тельна́я —
> Расформиро́вывается́.

The table[3] on p. 19 expresses, in percentages, the distribution of stress in the four-foot iambic lines contained in the work of twenty-eight poets ranging between the eighteenth and twentieth centuries. The numbers refer to the types of combination mentioned above.

There are several conclusions to be drawn from this table. Where two stresses are omitted in Russian, the two remaining ones are evenly spread over the second and fourth feet. The combination of stresses on the first and fourth feet is encountered rarely, and between the two

---

[1] See K. Taranovski, Руски дводелни ритмови, p. 86, n. 115.

[2] Quoted by G. Shengeli, Трактат о русском стихе, изд. 2-ое (М.-П., 1923), p. 32. The source is not given and it is possible that the quatrain was invented by Shengeli himself.

[3] Taken from L. Timofeev, Проблемы стиховедения, pp. 213–14.

stresses remains a block of five unstressed syllables, which is obviously an awkward arrangement.

Century	Number of lines examined	4 stresses	3 stresses			2 stresses	
		1	2	3	4	5	6
Eighteenth	7,052						
Lomonosov . . .	. .	64·0	1·5	14·5	19·5	0·3	0·2
Trediakovsky . .	. .	30·1	7·6	22·3	29·9	7·1	3·0
Sumarokov . . .	. .	29·6	3·4	22·9	37·7	4·1	2·3
Kheraskov . . .	. .	32·6	4·2	17·0	43·6	1·8	0·8
Iv. Dolgoruky . .	. .	41·3	2·1	5·6	48·4	2·3	0·3
Radishchev . . .	. .	36·4	0·6	16·6	43·2	2·0	1·2
Derzhavin . . .	. .	34·0	5·8	26·0	34·8	3·9	0·9
Nineteenth . . .	24,144						
Zhukovsky . . .	. .	27·0	4·0	13·0	44·5	9·0	2·5
Pushkin . . .	. .	27·5	6·5	8·5	47·5	10·0	0·2
Kozlov . . .	. .	34·4	4·6	4·2	50·8	5·7	0·3
Boratynsky . .	. .	28·1	9·4	1·7	51·3	9·4	0·1
Yazykov . . .	. .	17·3	4·1	2·5	64·0	12·4	0·2
Lermontov . . .	. .	30·0	6·0	6·5	50·0	7·0	0·5
Kar. Pavlova . .	. .	29·0	8·1	14·7	37·0	9·9	1·3
Tyutchev . . .	. .	25·0	6·5	9·4	44·3	14·2	0·5
Fet . . .	. .	27·1	11·1	7·0	43·4	11·2	0·2
Polezhaev . . .	. .	26·4	5·4	6·8	55·0	6·2	0·1
Nekrasov . . .	. .	26·6	6·3	8·9	48·1	10·0	0·1
Sluchevsky . .	. .	30·0	6·2	4·4	49·4	9·0	1·0
Lokhvitskaya . .	. .	35·8	6·2	3·8	45·1	9·1	—
Twentieth . . .	9,063						
In. Annensky . .	. .	20·0	8·0	5·0	50·0	15·0	1·0
Bryusov . . .	. .	31·3	8·1	16·3	38·5	5·3	0·5
Bely . . .	. .	15·5	7·5	20·5	38·5	16·5	1·5
Blok . . .	. .	29·2	8·2	13·5	41·2	7·9	—
Bunin . . .	. .	32·0	6·3	11·1	44·0	6·6	—
Ig. Severyanin . .	. .	29·0	8·2	3·0	43·0	16·4	0·4
Gumilev . . .	. .	28·3	7·6	8·9	42·9	10·3	2·0
Akhmatova . . .	. .	26·0	6·0	9·5	47·5	7·0	3·0

The complete realization of the metrical scheme, that is to say the maintenance of the four stresses, normally covers rather more than a quarter of the lines, but hardly ever reaches a third; any higher proportion would result in an effect too rigid and monotonous. This proportion was higher in the eighteenth century, notably in the work of Lomonosov, two-thirds of whose verse it affects, with a peak of 70·5 per cent. in his first odes.[1] Clearly, in his youth Lomonosov had taken the rules of versification too literally.

[1] An example is given on p. 21.

The most frequent departure from the metrical scheme is the omission of one of the four stresses, especially the stress on the third foot. This variant is found in nearly half the lines. The omission of the third stress gives added strength to the stress following, on the fourth foot, which is already strong. Since this last is obligatory, the omission of stress on the third foot never tends to cause too long and heavy a sequence of unstressed syllables.

The table also shows the preference of some authors for a particular combination of stresses as well as indicates the original and certainly deliberate accentuation of poets such as Yazykov or Bely.

The scrutiny of the distribution of accents century by century reveals a gradual decrease of the four-stress combination, which is compensated to some extent by a distinct increase of the two-stress, whereas the frequency of the three-stress combination is relatively stable. Thus the above table, arranged according to the centuries, gives the following percentages:[1]

Century	Number of lines	4 stresses 1	3 stresses			2 stresses	
			2	3	4	5	6
Eighteenth	7,052	38	4	18	36	3	1
				58		4	
Nineteenth	24,144	28·1	6·2	7·1	49	9	0·6
				62·3		9·6	
Twentieth	9,063	26·3	7·5	11·1	43·1	10·5	1·5
				61·7		12	

These statistics show the emergence of greater flexibility in the distribution of accents.

If the students of Russian verse have devoted a great

[1] This table is taken from L. Timofeev, op. cit., p. 213.

deal of attention to the four-foot iambic line, that is because this type of verse has been, and still is, most commonly
used in Russian poetry. Out of about 40,000 lines written
by Pushkin, more than 21,500 are composed in four-foot
iambics. The origin of this Russian metre raises no pro-
blems: Lomonosov took it over from German poetry,
especially from that of J. Ch. Günther.[1] Poets have chosen
the four-foot iambic line with which to express the kind of
poetry most representative of their period. Its prestige was
the same as that of heroic verse in English poetry. Except
for the initial and very brief popularity of the trochaic line,
a success due to the prevalence of the syllabic tradition,
the four-foot iambic throughout the second half of the
eighteenth century was employed in the ode. The first
example is Lomonosov's ode on the capture of Khotin,
composed in 1739. As a specimen, the nineteenth stanza of
this ode is given:

> Как в клуб змия себя крутит,
> Шипит, под камень жало кроет,
> Орёл когда шумя летит,
> И там парит, где ветр не воет;
> Превыше молний, бурь снегов,
> Зверей он видит, рыб, гадов.
> Пред Росской так дрожит Орлицей,
> Стесняет внутрь Хотин своих.
> Но что? в стенах ли может сих
> Пред сильной устоять царицей.

Except the last line, in which the second stress is omitted,
all other lines of this stanza bear the four metrical stresses.
This hammering metre is quite different from the smoother
rhythms of Lomonosov's later odes, and the odes of Derzhavin.[2]

---

[1] See K. Taranovski, op. cit., p. 70.
[2] A stanza of an ode by Derzhavin is given on p. 77.

The four-foot iambic line, however, is already found in the translations of Pastor Glück. Here is the opening of a hymn composed in alternate four- and three-foot iambic lines, together with the German original:[1]

> Allein Gott in der Höh sei Ehr
> Und Dank für seine Gnade,
> Darum, daß nun und nummermehr
> Uns rühren kann kein Schade.
> Ein Wohlgefall'n Gott an uns hat:
> Nun ist groß Fried ohn Unterlaß,
> All Fehde hat ein Ende.

> Бо́гу еди́ну бу́ди че́сть
> И похвала́ серде́чна;
> Отны́не бо́ нам бе́дства не́сть,
> Но ра́дость веко́вечна.
> Бо́г благода́тно на́с прия́л,
> Ми́р и поте́ху дарова́л,
> Весь ны́не стра́х сконча́лся.

At the beginning of the nineteenth century the four-foot iambic line was used for the fashionable new genres, the elegy and the epistle. Finally, it became the pattern for longer poems, whose models are still *Evgeny Onegin*,[2] *The Bronze Horseman*,[3] and *Poltava*[4] by Pushkin, and *The Demon*[5] by Lermontov.

The *five-foot iambic* line was used especially as a Russian imitation of the Shakespearian blank verse, though through

[1] See V. N. Peretts, op. cit., part ii, p. 69. The metre of this hymn is similar to that of *The Bridegroom* by Pushkin, of which a stanza is quoted on p. 79. Concerning the stress on the first syllable of the first, fifth, and sixth lines, see p. 38. It should be observed that J. W. Paus corrected the beginning of the first line in Еди́ну Бо́гу . . .

[2] Extracts are given on pp. 15, 77.

[3] An extract is given on p. 123.

[4] An extract is given on p. 38.   [5] An extract is given on p. 134.

the German intermediary of Schiller's plays, and occurred therefore in dramatic works. Like its English and German prototypes, this Russian line is rhymeless. It was very infrequent in the eighteenth century, and became popular only when Zhukovsky translated Schiller's *Maid of Orleans* in this measure in 1817–21. The same unrhymed five-foot iambic line was used by Pushkin to compose *Boris Godunov* and the 'little tragedies', and by A. K. Tolstoy and Ostrovsky to write their historical dramas. It has usurped the place of the six-foot iambic couplet, employed in eighteenth century tragedy.[1]

An example of this type of verse follows:

> Я с áглицким послóм покóнчил дéло;
> Но бóльно он тягýч и жиловáт:
> Торгóвые, вишь, льгóты англичáнам
> Всё подавáй! О льгóтах говорúть
> Мне с нúм не врéмя. Приглаcú егó
> К себé, к обéду, потолкýй с ним дéльно,
> И чтó он скáжет, тó мне донеcú.

> А. К. Толстóй, „Смерть Иоанна Грозного"

Zhukovsky revealed a preference for the five-foot iambic non-rhyming line and made use of it in several poems, such as the *Wandering Jew*, *Captain Bopp*, *The Tulip Tree*, and others.

As well, the five-foot rhyming iambic line has always been and is used still in lyric poetry.[2] Pushkin made use of it in *The Little House in Kolomna* (1830), and it is also the usual metre of the sonnet.[3]

As with the four-foot iambic, stress frequency-tables have been compiled concerning the Shakespearian line.

---

[1] See p. 25.
[2] See, for example, the quatrain of Blok quoted on p. 17.
[3] See p. 83.

Thus, in *Boris Godunov*, the stress combinations are as follows:[1]

Types of combination	Number of stresses in the line	Feet stressed					Percentage
1	5 stresses	1	2	3	4	5	19·2
2	4 stresses		2	3	4	5	7·3
3	—	1		3	4	5	9·3
4	—	1	2		4	5	3·3
5	—	1	2	3		5	30·7
6	3 stresses		2		4	5	1·1
7	—		2	3		5	9·2
8	—	1			4	5	1·4
9	—	1		3		5	19·0

The results are comparable with those of the four-foot iambic line. Combinations in which there is no stress on the penultimate—i.e. the fourth—foot, that is to say the combinations 5, 7, and 9, account for $30·7 + 9·2 + 19 = 58·9$ per cent., whereas in the four-foot iambic in the works of Pushkin the statistics read $47·5 + 10 + 0·2 = 57·7$ per cent. Equally noticeable is the preference for the balanced distribution of three stresses in the ninth combination, on the first, third, and fifth foot, $= 19$ per cent. Combinations with two stresses are practically non-existent. In the 'little tragedies' of Pushkin, nevertheless, three lines (0·2 per cent.) are found with stresses on the second and fifth feet.

The rhyming couplet in *six-foot iambic* verse was very frequent in the eighteenth century and in the first twenty years of the nineteenth; it predominated in tragedy and in epic. Although an essentially French verse-form, it was introduced into Russia by Lomonosov as an imitation of German poetry. The Russian poets, however, considered it as the Russian equivalent of the French Alexandrine.

[1] See G. Shengeli, op. cit., p. 170.

Of this type of poetry, Pushkin's *Angelo* (1833) represents
one of the last specimens, but not one of the best. As for
some other metres, Lomonosov had for the six-foot iambic
line, a precursor in a German poet working in Russia.
Here is the opening of an ode by J. W. Paus, celebrating
the triumphal entry into St. Petersburg of Peter the Great,
after the naval victory of 1714:[1]

> Небéсная рукá ‖ нам в и́стине чудéсна,
> Вели́кой шаутбейнáхт ‖ ужé ся возврати́л,
> Хоть нéдруг учини́л ‖ задéржки й мéста тéсна,
> А нáш Ирáклии ‖ вся мóнштры победи́л.

The passage which follows has been taken from an
eighteenth-century tragedy:

> Нетрóнут жáлостным ‖ позóрищем таки́м,
> Насы́ться, злóй тирáн, ‖ мучéнием мои́м!
> Когдá ты нáглые ‖ чтишь вáрварски устáвы;
> Рази́, влеки́ мои́ дýх, ‖ терзáй мои состáвы,
> Неви́нну крóвь мою ‖ подóбно ты пролéй,
> И рýки обагри́в, ‖ без сожалéнья, в нéй,
> Взведи́ на небесá ‖ окровавлéнны рýки,
> Чтоб ты́ избáвлен бы́л ‖ в том ми́ре вéчной мýки!
> Бог прáвый судия́, ‖ коли́ко óн ни щéдр;
> Не внéмлет óн моли́тв ‖ из тáртаровых нéдр.
> А. Сумарóков, „Дими́трий Самозванец", iv. 10 (1771)

The next example has been chosen from a poem of
Masonic inspiration:

> Труднéе всех наýк, ‖ некóнчимая в вéк,
> Для человéка есть ‖ наýка: человéк;
> Из ми́ра цéлого ‖ Всевы́шним сокращéнный,
> Он сáм во существé ‖ мир мáлый, совершéнный;
> Из твáрей всéх извлéк ‖ чистéйшее Госпóдь,
> И вдýнул дýх живóй ‖ в его небéсну плóть;
> Он тóчка срéдняя, ‖ он сéрдце всéй приро́ды,
> В нем вóздух и земля́, ‖ в нем скры́ты óгнь и вóды.
> М. Херáсков, „Влади́мир", viii (1785)

[1] V. N. Peretts, op. cit., part ii, pp. 144–5.

Later this Russian Alexandrine was replaced by the four-foot iambic line in long poems, and in verse-drama, which took the place of tragedy, it had to give way to the Shakespearian line.

But the six-foot iambic line, which is still common in modern poetry, is no longer connected with a recognized formula nor is it written in couplets. Here is an example occurring in the poetry of A. Akhmatova:

> Есть в бли́зости людей заве́тная черта́:
> Её не перейти́ влюблённости и стра́сти,
> Пусть в жу́ткой тишине́ слива́ются уста́
> И се́рдце рвётся от любви́ на ча́сти.

In this poem the last line of each quatrain has only five feet.

The iambic lines already examined—i.e. the four-, five-, and six-foot lines—remain the most common in modern poetry. Shorter lines are less frequent, as for example the *three-foot iambic* line, which is found in the poetry of Lomonosov and in that of his German precursors. A modern specimen follows:

> Свеже́ет. Ча́с усло́вный.
> С поле́й пошёл наро́д.
> Вся в ро́зовом, попо́вна
> Идёт на огоро́д.
>
> А. Бе́лый, „Попо́вна"

However, Nekrasov selected unrhymed three-foot iambic lines for the composition of his poem *Who is happy in Russia* (Кому на Руси́ жить хорошо).[1]

The *two-foot iambic* line is no more than an infrequent experiment in versification. The first stress is hardly ever omitted, as is shown by the following extract:

> Где сла́дкий шо́пот
> Мои́х лесо́в?
> Пото́ков ро́пот,
> Цветы́ луго́в?

[1] See p. 153.

Деревья го́лы;
Ковёр зимы́
Покры́л холмы́,
Луга́ и до́лы.

                                    Е. Боратынский

2. *The trochaic metre*

The beginning of the syllabic-accentual poetry in Russian was marked, as has been seen, by the preference for the trochaic line. This was due to the impulse of the syllabic tradition, an influence which flourished from 1735 to 1750. Later the trochaic verse was displaced by the iambic. Trochaic lines formed only 10·6 per cent. of the poetry of Pushkin,[1] and in the same way Boratynsky, from a total of 222 poems, wrote a mere 16 in trochaic, as against 195 in iambic metre.

In a poem written in trochaic lines, every odd syllable is strong and is in principle stressed, whereas every even syllable is weak and unstressed. All that has been said of the iambic line regarding the rhythmic pattern within the metrical scheme, can be equally applied to the trochaic line, wherein the same principle governs the omission of stress. Here is an example of a *four-foot trochaic* line, the most common type:

Отдыми́лся бо́й вчера́шний,	‿ – | ´ – | ´ – | ´ –
Вы́сох по́т, мета́лл просты́л,	´ – | ´ – | ´ – | ´
От око́пов па́хнет па́шней,	‿ – | ´ – | ´ – | ´ –
Ле́том, ми́рным и просты́м.	´ – | ´ – | ‿ – | ´

                        А. Твардовский, „Василий Тёркин"

The omission of stress in the first, third, and fourth lines will be noted.[2]

A stanza of a hymn in four-foot trochaic lines by Pastor

[1] N. V. Lapshina, Y. K. Romanovsky, B. I. Yarkho, Метрический справочник к стихотворениям Пушкина, М.-Л., 1934, p. 23.

[2] For an example of a four-foot trochaic quatrain with every stress marked, see p. 69.

Glück is given, together with the German original, as one
of the oldest examples of trochaic verse in Russian:[1]

Sei mein Retter, halt mich eben;
Wann ich sinke, sei mein Stab;
Sterb ich, Jesus sei mein Leben,
Wann ich schlafen geh, mein Grab;
Wann ich wieder aufersteh
Es so hilf mir, daß ich geh,
Da, wo Er in ew'gen Freuden
Wird Sein' Auserwählten weiden.

Бу́дь мне во́ждь, мой заступи́тель;
Ка́к паду́, ты подпира́й,
Умру́ — бу́дь мой ожини́тель,
Ка́к лежу́, ты покрыва́й.
Ка́к от сме́рти восстаю́,
Да́й, да ра́достен вхожу́
В ца́рства твоего́ пола́ты
Та́м блаже́нства добыва́ти.

Displaced by the iambic line in serious poetry, the
trochaic line took refuge in the less profound kinds of
poetry where it has succeeded in maintaining its position,
as for example in songs and in verse-tales. It became almost
the rule in imitations of folk-poetry. Consequently, the
four-foot trochaic rhymed line is found also in the tales
of Pushkin, in Ershov's *Little Hunchback-Horse*, and else-
where. The opening lines of the *Golden Cockerel* by Pushkin
follow:

Не́где, в тридевя́том ца́рстве,
В тридеся́том госуда́рстве,
Жи́л-был сла́вный ца́рь Дадо́н.
Смо́лоду был гро́зен о́н,
И сосе́дям то и де́ло
Наноси́л оби́ды сме́ло.

[1] V. N. Peretts, op. cit., part ii, p. 49. For the iambic foot at the beginning
of the third line, see p. 39.

Frequency-tables relating to the stresses in the four-foot trochaic line in Pushkin's tales are given below, the numbers corresponding to the equivalent variants of the four-foot iambic line in the table on p. 17.[1]

Types of combination	Number of stresses in the line	Feet stressed				Percentage
1	4 stresses	1	2	3	4	23·3
2	3 stresses		2	3	4	19·9
3	—	1		3	4	1·9
4	—	1	2		4	31·7
5	2 stresses		2		4	23·1
6	—	1			4	0·3

It is clear that, by comparison with the four-foot iambic line, the stress combinations of the trochaic line are and always have been more diverse. In the earliest odes of Lomonosov, the accentual monotony of the iambic line, in contrast with the wholly modern variety yielded by the trochaic line, is indeed striking. In these odes, the distribution of stress is as follows:

	In iambic lines per cent.	In trochaic lines per cent.
4 stresses	70·5	32
3 stresses	29·0	55
2 stresses	—	13

The trochaic metre, closely tied to the syllabic tradition, certainly benefited in matters of stress from the freedom which this latter convention enjoyed. On the other hand, the links of the trochaic measure with folk-poetry contributed also to its variety. In particular the tendency to develop the balanced two stresses—on the second and the

[1] See G. Shengeli, op. cit., p. 176.

fourth feet—may be explained in this way.[1] This combination accounts for 13 per cent. in the earliest odes of Lomonosov, and for 23·1 per cent. in Pushkin's trochaic tales, as against 10 per cent. in Pushkin's four-foot iambic line.

Poets of the nineteenth century ceased to make a distinction between the inferior and superior genres in Russian poetry, or rather they no longer made the choice of metre dependent on this distinction, and by this method they rehabilitated the trochaic line and contributed to its relative success.

Trochaic measures other than four-foot are inclined to be rare. Of the variants, the *five-foot trochaic* line occupies the first place. It owes its popularity from the second half of the nineteenth century onwards to imitations of foreign models and notably to German lyric poetry. It is worth noting that Pushkin did not compose a single line in five-foot trochaics. One celebrated poem of Lermontov, of which the opening lines follow, has contributed to its success:

> Выхожу́ оди́н я на доро́гу:
> Сквозь тума́н кремни́стый пу́ть блести́т;
> Но́чь тиха́, пусты́ня вне́млет Бо́гу,
> И звезда́ с звездо́ю говори́т.

This poem, set to music, became a romance known all over Russia. In general, the four- and five-foot trochaics were frequently used in romances. Those that go by the name of 'chansons tsiganes' (цыга́нские пе́сни) often use this metre, as in the following example:

> Мой костёр в тума́не све́тит,
> И́скры га́снут на лету́;
> Но́чью нас никто́ не встре́тит —
> Мы прости́мся на мосту́.
>
> Я. Полонский

---

[1] See K. Taranovski, op. cit., p. 53.

In a Russian five-foot trochaic line, besides the strong
fifth stress, which is of course compulsory, the next strong-
est stress is the second, which is nearly always maintained,
as in the example quoted.

The *six-foot trochaic* line, with a strong caesura after the
third foot, although used by Lomonosov and Sumarokov,
has remained a rare metre. Polonsky used it for the poem
Кузнечик музыкант, and Nekrasov for some minor poems.
It had, in the second half of the nineteenth century, a certain, though limited, success with second-rate poets. An
example is given in the last stanza of Nekrasov's poem *The
Forgotten Village* (Забытая деревня):

> Наконéц, однáжды ‖ середи́ доро́ги
> Шестернéю цу́гом ‖ показáлись дро́ги:
> На дрогáх высо́ких ‖ гро́б стои́т дубо́вый,
> А в гробу́-то бáрин, ‖ а за гро́бом — но́вый.
> Стáрого отпéли, ‖ но́вый слёзы вы́тер,
> Сéл в свою карéту ‖ — и уéхал в Пи́тер.

The ballad likewise made use of the trochaic metre,
usually combining four feet in odd lines and three feet in
even lines. Historically, this type of verse is derived from
the Russian-Polish Alexandrine of the syllabic poetry,
which ultimately acquired an almost perfect trochaic
cadence. This thirteen-syllable Alexandrine was split by
a strong masculine caesura into two hemistichs, which, in
the ballad-verse, became respectively the odd line of seven
syllables and the even line of six syllables.[1] The opening
lines of Zhukovsky's ballad *Svetlana*, which is composed in
this measure, follow:

> Рáз в крещéнский вечеро́к
> Дéвушки гадáли:
> За воро́та башмачо́к,
> Сня́в с ноги́, бросáли.

[1] See K. Taranovski, op. cit., pp. 47–48.

The same metre, but with a constant feminine rhyme, was preferred by the Ukrainian poet Shevchenko.[1]

The pure *three-foot trochaic* line, although it was introduced by Sumarokov, has remained a rare metre. It is found, for example, in the following poem by Lermontov, inspired by Goethe's poem *Über allen Gipfeln ist Ruh . . .* :

> Го́рные верши́ны
> Спя́т во тьме́ ночно́й;
> Ти́хие доли́ны
> По́лны све́жей мгло́й;
> Не пыли́т доро́га,
> Не дрожа́т листы́ . . .
> Подожди́ немно́го,
> Отдохнёшь и ты́.

The *two-foot trochaic* line is even rarer than the two-foot iambic line. Here is a specimen:

> Всё черне́е
> Сво́д надзвёздный;
> Всё страшне́е
> Во́ют бе́здны;
> Ве́тр свисти́т,
> Гро́м греми́т,
> Мо́ре сто́нет —
> Пу́ть далёк . . .
> То́нет, то́нет
> Мой челно́к!
>
> А. Полежаев, „Песнь погибающего пловца"

Since the eighteenth century the trochaic line has served for imitations of Russian folk-poetry, whose cadence, in fact, is generally trochaic, with a dactylic clausula (кла́у-зула), which may easily spread over two words. These two characteristics of folk-poetry were used by imitators in the eighteenth century in order to suggest verse of a 'popular' kind: a four-foot trochaic line, ending with a dactyl, and

---

[1] Concerning the Russian imitations of this metre, see p. 39.

rhymeless ($\acute{-} - | \acute{-} - | \acute{-} - | \acute{-} - -$). It was in this measure that Karamzin wrote his Илья Муромец, in 1794. About the metre, the author himself remarks: В рассуждении меры скажу, что она совершенно Русская. Почти все наши старинные песни сочинены такими стихами, which is somewhat exaggerated. An example follows:

> Кто́ сей ви́тязь, богаты́рь младо́й?
> Он подо́бен Ма́ю кра́сному:
> Ро́зы а́лые с лиле́ями
> Расцвета́ют на лице́ его.
> Он подо́бен ми́рту не́жному:
> То́нок, пря́м и велича́в собой.

Evidently Karamzin has grasped the principle of the dactylic clausula spread over two words. But this is practically the only detail linking this line to the Russian epic song, the *bylina*, which Karamzin intended to imitate. Apart from this, his poem, which sets out to conform to sophisticated taste, is very far from popular tradition. The same metre was used for similar unsuccessful imitations of folk-poetry by Kheraskov in *Bakhariana* and by Pushkin in *Bova*.

Koltsov made use of this metrical formula as well, in which the absence of stress on the first syllable is another characteristic borrowed from folk-poetry. An example follows:

> На заре́ тума́нной ю́ности
> Всей душо́й люби́л я ми́лую.
> Был у не́й в глаза́х небе́сный свет;
> На лице́ горе́л любви́ огонь.

This poet also used two other trochaic metres in his imitations of folk-poetry, both without rhyme.

One is a three-foot trochaic line with trochaic clausula:

> Ве́село на па́шне; $\acute{-} - | - - | \acute{-} -$
> Ну́! тащи́ся, си́вка! $\acute{-} - | \acute{-} - | \acute{-} -$
> Я́ сам-дру́г с тобо́ю, $\acute{-} - | \acute{-} - | \acute{-} -$
> Слуга́ и хозя́ин. $- \acute{-} | - - | \acute{-} -$

Вéсело я лáжу	´– | –– | ´–
Бóрону и сóху,	´– | –– | ´–
Телéгу готóвлю,	–´ | –– | ´–
Зёрна насыпáю.	´– | –– | ´–

The two characteristics of this metre are the frequent omission of the medium stress and the frequent replacement of the first foot by an iambus, of which the last line of the first and the third line of the second couplet show examples.[1]

His other metre includes a cadence frequent in popular songs, and is a three-foot trochaic line, of which the third foot is truncated, leaving a stress at the end of the line. The first and third stresses are weakened, if not omitted, with the result that the line normally consists of a group of five syllables with a strong accent on the third syllable. This weakening of the two lateral stresses applies even when the beats fall on autonomous words which in lines similar, but not meant to be sung, would have received full stress value. Here is an example:

Ся́ду я за стóл	´– | –– | ´
Да подýмаю:	–– | ´– | –
Как на свéте жи́ть	–– | ´– | ⌣
Одинóкому?	–– | ´– | –
Нет у мóлодца	–– | ´– | –
Молодóй жены́,	–– | ´– | ⌣
Нет у мóлодца	–– | ´– | –
Дрýга вéрного . . .	⌣– | ´– | –

The whole of this metre can be explained only in terms of song. Koltsov intended that his poetry should be sung. And in fact his poems have been set to music more frequently than those of any other Russian poet. For example,

---

[1] Concerning this phenomenon, see p. 39.

the poem whose opening has just been quoted has inspired
nine different composers.

Trochaic cadence with six stresses is found in some
genres of folk-poetry, for example in North-Russian lamen-
tations (причита́ния). It is also that of the text accompany-
ing the well-known dance melody, called Кома́ринский
мужи́к. Its imitation in Russian poetry gives a six-foot
trochaic line without caesura, quite different from the
same line with caesura, examined above. Here is, as an
example, the second stanza of a poem by Nikitin:

> У меня́ зимо́й в избу́шке сы́ро, хо́лодно,
> Ма́ть-стару́ха привере́длива, причу́длива,
> Сёстры злы́, а я́ голо́вушка разгу́льная,
> Мно́го го́ря ты́ со мно́ю понате́рпишься.

The rhymeless line and the dactylic clausula are other
popular features of this poem.

3. *General remarks on binary metres*

As has been seen, Russian allows the following deviations
from the metrical scheme in binary verse.

1. Omission of stress on strong syllables if a word is
spread over more than one foot and would incur more than
one stress.

2. Omission of stress on strong syllables when these
occur in certain words, such as prepositions, conjunctions,
and particles, which are usually unstressed.

3. Omission of stress on certain monosyllables and
disyllables, such as adverbs and various kinds of pronoun,
which are normally unstressed, but which in certain circumstances can be given stress. These circumstances are
generally determined by the meaning.

The variability of stress is further increased by the fact
that in every kind of metre, the ternary included, stress on
the strong syllables can be either strengthened or weakened

as logic or emphasis requires. But such cases, which depend solely on consideration of rhythm or syntax, are irrelevant, strictly speaking, to the metrical pattern.

This variability of stress gives Russian verse its rhythm and its individuality. It is the task of each poet to find, within the limits of a given metre, the rhythm best adapted to his theme. Questions of vocabulary and euphony apart, that is where, in the main, the art of Russian versification lies.

Normally in Russian prose the proportion of accented syllables to the total number of syllables is 1 to 2·8. An iambic or a trochaic metre, fully developed, would bring this proportion to 1 to 2, which would give an excess of accented syllables. The omission of accents allows the rhythm of binary lines to reach the accentual frequency of the everyday language and even to adopt a very similar form, whereas the variability in the number of syllables in the unstressed intervals which results from the omission of accent brings the rhythm of binary lines even closer to the cadence of spoken Russian. These factors doubtless account for the great popularity of binary metres in Russian poetry.

One may well wonder what remains of a Russian metrical scheme, if it is constantly undermined by the poet's individual rhythm. Certainly, some students of Russian verse have thought it possible and even desirable to abandon metrical schemes completely and to work with existing rhythmic patterns as their sole basis. For them the metrical schemes are mere conventions without real content.

However, such an idea is indefensible, not only because, with no substitute for the metrical scheme, it leads to chaos in the system of versification, but because it tends to obscure the fact that individual rhythms in no way destroy the metrical scheme, which is present, though hidden, in the verse. The stress that is omitted continues to exercise a potential influence, especially if it is remembered that one line taken on its own is not enough to establish the cadence of a poem; two lines at least are needed to establish this with certainty. Now the rhythmic pattern of two neighbouring lines may not be the same, generally it is not, and this facilitates the quick comprehension of the metre of the poem. The following example bears out this statement.

In Lermontov's poem *The Demon*, at the end of the ninth stanza in the first part, occurs the following line which, incidentally, is not entirely successful:

Да он и не взял бы забвенья.

This line may be stressed in two ways, neither of which violates Russian usage:

Да о́н и не взя́л бы забве́нья,

giving an amphibrachic line: $- \acute- - \mid - \acute- - \mid - \acute- -$; or

Да о́н и не́ взял бы забве́нья,

giving an iambic line with the stress on the third foot omitted:

$$- \acute- \mid - \acute- \mid - - \mid - \acute- \mid -.$$

Although the second type of accentuation may be less common than the first, at least in contemporary usage, it gives the cadence required, if this line is compared with the preceding one, which is clearly iambic in structure:

Забы́ть? — Забве́нья не́ дал Бо́г,
Да о́н и не́ взял бы забве́нья.

Consideration of the whole stanza reveals not the slightest possibility of any other accentuation. In other words, a single line does not decide the metre of the whole passage, and though not apparent, the metrical scheme dominates every syllabic-accentual poem. But there is more to it than that. In binary verse the metrical scheme contains a stable element which remains constant, whatever the rhythmic pattern of the line. This element is the arrangement of weak syllables. That is too readily forgotten, because it is stress that normally holds the attention.

In fact, whether in an iambic metre strong (even) syllables can be stressed or not, weak (odd) syllables are *always* unstressed. Exactly the same applies, *mutatis mutandis*, to the trochaic metre. That is the simplest definition of binary metre in Russian. It will doubtless be considered somewhat surprising that a metre should be defined in terms of its weak syllables. It would be wrong, however, to underestimate the importance of such a definition.

It may happen, however, that in an iambic line the first syllable commands the stress; in such a case, it is always a monosyllable and the stress is purely emphatic. This supplementary stress can be termed hypermetrical, and its occurrence indirectly influences the metrical structure of the line. Some examples follow:

> Белеет парус одинокий
> В тумане моря голубом . . .
> Что ищет он в стране далёкой?
> Что кинул он в краю родном?
>
> М. Лермонтов, ,,Парус"

> Швед, русский — колет, рубит, режет;
> Бой барабанный, клики, скрежет;
> Гром пушек, топот, ржанье, стон,
> И смерть и ад со всех сторон.
>
> А. Пушкин, ,,Полтава"

It happens also that the first foot in an iambic line can be replaced by a trochaic foot: in such a case, the first word of the line may also be a disyllable. Now this inversion is essentially a metrical device which normally has no connexion with emphatic stress. In the passage from *Pol-*

tava quoted above, the second line contains an example.
Other examples in four- and five-foot iambics follow:

> Со вре́менем сей до́м, я зна́ю,
> Кра́сен мне бу́дет платежо́м.
>
> И. Долгору́кий, „Ками́н в Москве́"

> Три ра́за преклони́ться до́лу,
> Се́мь — осени́ть себя́ кресто́м.
>
> А. Бло́к

> Я зна́ю, что дере́вьям, а не на́м,
> Дано́ вели́чье соверше́нной жи́зни.
> На ла́сковой земле́, сестре́ звезда́м,
> Мы́ — на чужби́не, а они́ — в отчи́зне.
>
> Н. Гумиле́в, „Дере́вья"

If this inversion is applied systematically in a poem it
occasions a new metre.[1]

Conversely, in a trochaic poem the first foot can be replaced by an iambic foot, which is, in fact, simply a metrical device:

> И несме́ло у него́
> Про́сят: „Ну́-ка, на́ ночь
> Расскажи́ ещё́ чего́,
> Васи́лий Ива́ныч".
>
> А. Твардо́вский, „Васи́лий Тёркин"

The iambic foot occurs in the last line.

This is a practice commonly adopted in imitations of
popular songs and has already been mentioned in connexion with Koltsov's poetry.[2]

In the Ukrainian poems of Shevchenko, which are
written in alternate four-foot and three-foot trochaic lines
with feminine rhyme, the substitution of the iambic foot
for the initial trochaic foot in the shorter line is a device

---

[1] See chapter on accentual verse, p. 94.
[2] See p. 34. The 'popular' appeal of the passage quoted will be
observed.

frequently used; and similarly in Russian poems which imitate this metre, as in the following example:

> Опана́с гляди́т карти́ной
> В папа́хе косма́той,
> Шу́ба с ме́ртвого равви́на
> Под Го́мелем сня́та.
> Шу́ба — пла́тье меховóе —
> Распа́хнута — жа́рко!
> Фре́нч англи́йского покрóя
> Добы́т за Вапня́ркой.
> На руке́ с нага́йкой кре́пкой
> Жеребя́чье мы́ло,
> Револьве́р виси́т на це́пке
> От паникади́ла.
>
>   Э. Багри́цкий, ,,Ду́ма про Опана́са"

The iambic foot is substituted for the trochaic in the second, fourth, sixth, and eighth lines. Thus an interval of two syllables is created between the two stresses, and these modified lines take the form of two amphibrachs: $- \acute{} - \,|\, - \acute{} -$. This rhythmic change is one of the attractions of Shevchenko's verse.

To sum up, the metre of binary verse might be described as leaving unstressed the weak syllables, the odd ones in the iambic line, and the even ones in the trochaic, and in maintaining or omitting stresses on strong syllables.

The omission of stresses allows binary verse the possibility of unstressed intervals either of one, or of three, syllables. That produces, as has been seen, many variants in the rhythmic pattern of a single poem. Certain Russian theorists, particularly those who consider the foot as the real unit of the verse, have attempted to label all these variants with the help of a terminology borrowed from Greek versification. Thus, a disyllabic foot without stress, or, perhaps, with the stress omitted, is called *pyrrhic* (пирри́хий: $- -$). Sometimes a foot with stress and a nearby foot without—a pyrrhic foot—are combined in a metrical unit of four syllables called a *paeon* (пэо́н); and there is therefore a distinction between the first paeon (пэо́н пе́рвый: $\acute{-}---$), the second paeon (пэо́н второ́й: $-\acute{-}--$), the third paeon (пэо́н тре́тий: $--\acute{-}-$), and the fourth paeon (пэо́н четвёртый: $---\acute{-}$). When the first syllable of an iambic foot is stressed, these theorists speak of a *spondee* (спонде́й: $\acute{-}\,\acute{-}$). Similarly, the trochaic foot replacing the iambic foot forms with the following iambic foot a *choriambus* (хория́мб: $\acute{-}--\acute{-}$). The expressions *ionic majore* (ио́ник нисходя́щий: $\acute{-}\,\acute{-}--$) and *ionic minore* (ио́ник восходя́щий: $--\acute{-}\,\acute{-}$) are also in use. The present author thought it preferable to avoid this terminology which makes a useless sacrifice of the line to the foot. The sharp distinction made instead between the metrical scheme and its rhythmic pattern seems both simpler and more in keeping with the facts of Russian verse.

4. *Comparison with German and English verse*

For a clearer perception of the distinctive qualities of the Russian binary metres it is useful to compare them with similar metres in German and English poetry. A detailed comparison is, of course, outside the scope of this study and this section will, therefore, be limited to a brief survey of the essential basis of binary metres, which is the distribution of stress.

The special characteristic of Russian binary metre is the marked difference between the metrical scheme and its rhythmic pattern. This difference is due to the weakening and disappearance of certain stresses on strong syllables; the accentuation of weak syllables is exceptional, and in practice occurs only in the initial foot.

How do German and English behave in this respect?

In *German,* words are shorter than in Russian, and compound words incur stress upon each of their elements, with the result that in German verse there are markedly fewer reasons for omitting stress. Thus a certain impulse communicated by the stress prevails, affecting even the little auxiliary words which, in Russian, are normally unstressed; moreover, long words, such as compound words, readily incur a secondary stress (*Nebenton*). Consequently, the metrical scheme is almost always developed rhythmically in German verse, so that stress may be weakened, but seldom disappears. To a Russian ear, the recitation of a German poem sounds always over-scanned and, for that reason, monotonous. Here is a specimen, composed in a five-foot iambic measure:

> Am Jüngsten Tág, wenn die Posáunen schállen,
> Und álles áus ist mít dem Érdelében,
> Sind wír verpflíchtet Réchenschaft zu gében
> Von jédem Wórt, das únnütz úns entfállen.

> Goethe, *Warnung*

This quatrain, read in the German tradition, introduces all the metrical stresses save two. Among these stresses, there are some strong ones that could equally well appear in Russian. But there are also some weak ones which would disappear in Russian, but which in German are only lightened. Examples are the second stress on *Érdelében*, the stress on the auxiliary word *mit*, and stresses on the ambiguous words *aus, wir,* and *uns* that Russian would not keep in similar circumstances. Only two stresses are omitted: on the auxiliary word *die* in the first line, and on the last syllable of the word *Réchenschaft*. Generally speaking, the gradation in the strength of the stresses combined with the difference in quantity between long and short vowels, a difference unknown in Russian, enriches German prosody and diminishes the rigidity of its scansion.[1]

The quatrain quoted, read in the Russian manner, would shock a German by its lack of firmness, and, undoubtedly, by its prosaic effect.

In *English*, words are even shorter than in German, and long words normally have a secondary stress. It follows that the removal of stresses in English is less common than in Russian. But the abundance of monosyllables in the English vocabulary often means that significant monosyllables follow one another, each of them bearing its semantic stress. The result is that in English verse weak syllables may receive a stress, disyllables as well as monosyllables. Here is a Spenserian stanza as illustration, composed in five-foot iambics, with the last line containing six feet:

1   And Árdennes[2] wáves abóve them her gréen leáves,
2   Déwy with Náture's teár-dróps, as they páss—
3   Gríeving, if aúght inánimate e'ér gríeves,
4   Óver the únretúrning bráve,—alás!
5   Ere évening to be tródden like the gráss
6   Which nów beneáth them, but abóve sháll grów
7   In its néxt vérdure, whén this fíery máss
8   Of líving Válour, rólling on the fóe
9   And búrning with hígh Hópe, shall móulder cóld and lów.

                                    Byron, *Childe Harold*, iii. 27

In this passage, one long word, *únretúrning*, takes two stresses, but not the word *inánimate*, which has only one stress. Six lines have the five stresses required by the metre. The last line has six stresses; one, the eighth, has four

---

[1] The difference in the rhythmic pattern between the Russian and the German verse is clearly illustrated by many diagrams in K. Taranovski's Руски дводелни ритмови, especially by those on pp. 74, 94, 195, 205, 224, 280.

[2] For rhythmical reasons the stress *Árdennes*, in this line, is to be preferred to the correct stress *Ardénnes*.

stresses; and one, the fifth, three. But these stresses can be moved so as to fall on the weak syllables, which are odd ones. As a result, two stresses sometimes follow one another: *gréen leáves*; *teár-dróps*; *e'ér gríeves*; *néxt vérdure*; *hígh Hópe*. The sixth line offers three consecutive stresses: *abóve sháll gŕow*. Three disyllabic words incur the fall of a stress on the weak syllable in the foot: *déwy*, *gríeving* and *óver*. They are found at the beginning of the line and so offer a trochaic opening, which happens occasionally in Russian also.[1] Five cases of the omission of stress can be detected on auxiliary words: on *as* in the second line, *to* and *like* in the fifth line, *but* in the sixth line, and *on* in the eighth line. One stress is omitted in a long word: *inánimate*.

It is the displacement of stress which is the chief characteristic of English binary metre. Non-metrical stresses are common also, and the stress is sometimes omitted, though this occurs least often. All these deviations gradually wear away the metre, and syntactical stress tends to replace metrical stress. In consequence, English verse seems to drift steadily towards a syllabism of the French type by producing a line composed of accentual groups dominated by semantic stress. Even more than in German, differences in intensity, in quantity, and also in the pitch of the stressed vowels play a part in the rhythmic pattern of English verse. Therefore, in English, much more than in Russian, the recitation of a poem is dependent on individual interpretation.

A comparison of the three systems shows that German binary verse stays closest to the metrical scheme. Russian verse deviates from it by the *number* of stresses, and English verse by their *distribution*.

French verse conforms to rules that are too different for comparison with syllabic-accentual verse to be useful.

[1] See p. 38.

Sometimes, however, a distribution of stresses occurs which accidentally coincides with one binary metre or another; but this is never more than an accident which is unlikely to be repeated in neighbouring lines. When this accident occurs French verse bears a resemblance to Russian because of its suppressed metrical stresses. Here is an unusual example of a French quatrain which seems to the Russian reader to be composed of four-foot trochaics which are perfectly regular:

> Honte à toi qui la première
> M'as appris la trahison,
> Et d'horreur et de colère
> M'as fait perdre la raison!
>
> A. de Musset, *La Nuit d'Octobre*

III. TERNARY METRES

Ternary metres are less frequent than binary metres in Russian poetry. They comprise three variants:

1. The dactylic metre, based on the dactylic foot ($\acute{-}\, -\, -$).

2. The amphibrachic metre, based on the amphibrachic foot ($-\, \acute{-}\, -$).

3. The anapaestic metre, based on the anapaestic foot ($-\, -\, \acute{-}$).

The term amphibrach is seldom used outside Russia. In English and German versification amphibrachic lines are regarded either as dactylic with anacrusis:[1] $-\, |\, \acute{-}\, -\, -\, |\, \acute{-}\, -\, -$; or as anapaestic preceded by an iambic foot: $-\, \acute{-}\, |\, -\, -\, \acute{-}\, |\, -\, -\, \acute{-}$. Specimens of this type of versification are found early, in fact from the eighteenth century onwards. Lomonosov mentions them in his *Epistle* in 1739; Trediakovsky, too, in his *Treatise* in 1752, tried to endow Russian poetry with a choice of forms comparable with that existing in Western

[1] Concerning this term, see p. 57.

European poetry. Even J. W. Paus used amphibrachic lines.[1] Nevertheless, throughout the eighteenth century, ternary verses remained the exception. In the work of Derzhavin only twenty-five dactylic and nine amphibrachic poems are found, and not a single poem in anapaestic lines. The preference given to the dactylic line is explained by the fact that this metre was used in imitations of the classical hexameter.[2]

Ternary metres began to achieve popularity only at the beginning of the nineteenth century. In the poetry of Pushkin, who in so many ways still belongs to the eighteenth century, lines of ternary metres are still exceptional and account for only 1·5 per cent. of his entire verse. They are more frequent in the poetry of Zhukovsky and Lermontov; in Nekrasov's poetry they attain 40 per cent., and account for half the total output of the symbolist poet Bryusov.[3]

Unlike binary verse, the rhythmic pattern in ternary verse is much closer to the metrical scheme. As a general rule, the two notions are even identical, which is not hard to understand. The strong syllables, in these lines, are separated by two weak syllables and the omission of a stress would result in a sequence of five unstressed syllables, a hiatus which the rhythm would hardly tolerate. Such a sequence has been shown to be impracticable in binary verse. Thus the stress in ternary verse may be weakened, but, as a rule, it is not omitted.[4] On the other hand certain weak syllables may receive a stress not demanded by the metre.

Ternary metre was exploited largely in the romances, of which Fet, A. K. Tolstoy, Polonsky, Koltsov, and other

---

[1] See p. 49.   [2] See p. 47.
[3] These figures are taken from B. V. Tomashevsky, Теория литературы: Поэтика, 5-ое изд., М.-Л., 1930, p. 119.
[4] For the exception in dactylic verse, see p. 53.

poets of the mid-nineteenth century have furnished numerous examples.

1. *The dactylic metre*

As has been said already, the dactylic line is the com-
monest among the ternary metres. It is also the first to
have found its way into Russian poetry. In the poetry of
Nekrasov, who used ternary metres a great deal, dactylic,
anapaestic, and amphibrachic lines are found in the following proportions: 4, 3, 1; and in that of Fet the proportions are: 4, 3, 3.

Here is an example of the *four-foot dactylic* line:

> Тучки небесные, ‖ вечные странники,
> Степью лазурною, ‖ цепью жемчужною,
> Мчитесь вы, будто как ‖ я же, изгнанники,
> С милого севера ‖ в сторону южную.

М. Лермонтов

$$
\begin{aligned}
&\acute{-}\,-\,-\;|\;\acute{-}\,-\,-\;|\;\acute{-}\,-\,-\;|\;\acute{-}\,-\,- \\
&\acute{-}\,-\,-\;|\;\acute{-}\,-\,-\;|\;\acute{-}\,-\,-\;|\;\acute{-}\,-\,- \\
&\acute{-}\,-\,-\;|\;\acute{-}\,-\,-\;|\;\acute{-}\,-\,-\;|\;\acute{-}\,-\,- \\
&\acute{-}\,-\,-\;|\;\acute{-}\,-\,-\;|\;\acute{-}\,-\,-\;|\;\acute{-}\,-\,-
\end{aligned}
$$

Clearly, in these lines the metrical scheme is realized
fully in the rhythm. As is usually the case with ternary
metres, there is no deviation from the metre.

The *six-foot dactylic* line was regarded as the Russian
equivalent of the classical hexameter. Taken from German
poetry, in particular from that of Klopstock and Goethe,
this metre was quite frequent in imitations of Greek verse
at the end of the eighteenth century and at the beginning
of the nineteenth, but it died out in the second half of the
nineteenth century. Verse of this type is rhymeless and a
weak caesura occurs within the third foot. An example
follows:

> В колокол, мирно дремавший, ‖ с налёта тяжёлая бомба
> Грянула. С треском кругом от ‖ неё разлетелись осколки.

Óн же вздрогнýл — и к нарóду ‖ могýчие мéдные звýки
Вдáль потеклú, негодýя, ‖ гудя́ и на бóй созывáя.

А. К. Толстóй

```
⏑́ − − | ⏑́ − − | ⏑́ − ‖ − | ⏑́ − − | ⏑́ − − | ⏑́ −
⏑́ − − | ⏑́ − − | ⏑́ − ‖ − | ⏑́ − − | ⏑́ − − | ⏑́ −
⏑́ − − | ⏑́ − − | ⏑́ − ‖ − | ⏑́ − − | ⏑́ − − | ⏑́ −
⏑́ − − | ⏑́ − − | ⏑́ − ‖ − | ⏑́ − − | ⏑́ − − | ⏑́ −
```

More often, though, imitation of the classical hexameter leads to a mixed line, the dactylo-trochaic.[1]

2. *The amphibrachic metre*

The amphibrachic metre is predominant in Russian ballad, which generally combines lines of four and three feet. This type of amphibrachic verse was made fashionable by Zhukovsky. Pushkin used it in *The Song of Oleg the Wise*. But it was also used in others forms of poetry, of which an example follows:

И   éсли загрóбная жúзнь нам данá,
   Óн, здéшней вполнé отдышáвший
И в звýчных, глубóких отзы́вах сполнá
   Всё дóльное дóлу отдáвший,
К Предвéчному лёгкой душóй возлетúт,
И в нéбе земнóе егó не смутúт.

Е. Боратынский, „ На смерть Гете "

```
− ⏑́ − | − ⏑́ − | − ⏑́ − | − ⏑́·
− ⏑́ − | − ⏑́ − | − ⏑́ −
− ⏑́ − | − ⏑́ − | − ⏑́ − | − ⏑́
− ⏑́ − | − ⏑́ − | − ⏑́ −
− ⏑́ − | − ⏑́ − | − ⏑́ − | − ⏑́
− ⏑́ − | − ⏑́ − | − ⏑́ − | − ⏑́
```

The same regularity and the same identity between rhythm and metre as in dactylic verse may be observed here.

[1] See p. 99.

Yet there are occasional examples in which the first syllable may take an emphatic stress. In the stanza quoted above, this happens with the word он at the beginning of the second line.[1]

The oldest amphibrachic poem seems to be an ode which J. W. Paus composed in 1711, in combined four- and two-foot lines, on the betrothal of Peter the Great's son, the Tsarevich Alexis. The opening follows:[2]

> Преслáвные вéщи в конéц достизáют
> В желáемой счáстлив и дóброй приклáд.
> Неблáгополýчная ся́ отлучáют,
> Понéже сам Бóг вся упрáвити ря́д.
> Кто хрáбро трудúтся,
> Томý укрепúтся
> У́м, дýх и рукá;
> Тот вся́ побеждáет
> И чéсть получáет,
> Корóна в конéц тому дáрствуется́.

3. *The anapaestic metre*

The anapaestic metre seems to have been the last to establish itself among the ternary metres. An example follows, composed in alternate lines of four and three feet:

> Это бы́ло не рáз, это бýдет не рáз,
> В нашей бúтве, глухóй и упóрной:
> Как всегдá, ты вчерá от меня́ отреклáсь,
> Зáвтра, знáю, вернёшься покóрной.
>
>   Н. Гумилев

```
_ _ ʹ | _ _ ʹ | _ _ ʹ | _ _ ʹ
_ _ ʹ | _ _ ʹ | _ _ ʹ | _
_ _ ʹ | _ _ ʹ | _ _ ʹ | _ _ ʹ
ʹ _ ʹ | _ _ ʹ | _ _ ʹ | _
```

As with the previous metres, the rhythmic design is extremely regular.

---

[1] Concerning this stress, see p. 52.
[2] V. N. Peretts, op. cit., part ii, p. 135.

The first syllable of an anapaestic line may take a hyper-metrical stress. In the stanza quoted above, this happens with the word за́втра at the beginning of the last line.[1]

The two-foot anapaestic line is suited perfectly to romances. Accordingly, poets who, like Koltsov, excel in writing songs, very readily make use of it. A specimen follows:

Так и рвётся душа́	– – ´ | – – ´
Из груди́ молодо́й!	– – ´ | – – ´
Хо́чет во́ли она́,	´ – ´ | – – ´
Про́сит жи́зни друго́й!	´ – ´ | – – ´

А. Кольцов, ,,Песня"

In this quatrain the third and fourth lines take a non-metrical stress on the first syllable. The poem, rather mediocre, of which the quatrain quoted is the opening, has been set to music by twenty different composers.

There exists another variant of the same metre, in which each even line is a syllable shorter and so forms a one-foot anapaestic line, with a dactylic ending. In practice, this even line of five syllables is identical with the five-syllable —i.e. two-foot—trochaic line.[2] The rendering of the song may in fact make us hesitate between an anapaestic or a trochaic interpretation of this line. The same poet used this variant in his imitations of popular songs:

Оседла́ю коня́,	– – ´ | – – ´
Коня́ бы́строва,	– – ´ | – –
Я помчу́сь, полечу́	– – ´ | – – ´
Ле́гче со́кола.	– – ´ | – –

4. *General remarks on ternary metres*

It has been shown that the rhythmic pattern of ternary lines is, generally, identical with the metrical scheme. That is true to the extent that, in this type of verse, one word

---

[1] Concerning this stress, see p. 52.   [2] See p. 34.

may even take two stresses if it is sufficiently long to spread
over two feet. In such a case, the metrical stress other than
the usual stress is necessarily weakened, but is still perceptible. Examples of this are rare, but illustrations are given
in the following quotations taken from three-foot anapaestic
poems:

> Где с полу́госуда́рства дохо́ды
> Получа́ет замо́рский това́р.
>> Н. Некрасов, ,,Убогая и наряднáя"

> Я́, я́, я́. Что за ди́кое сло́во!
> Неуже́ли вон то́т — это я́?
> Ра́зве ма́ма люби́ла тако́го,
> Желтосе́рого, по́луседо́го
> И всезна́ющего как змея́?
>> В. Ходасевич, ,,Перед зеркалом"[1]

And again in the same poem:

> На траги́ческие разгово́ры
> Научи́лся молча́ть и шути́ть.

The three illustrations below are taken from a three-foot
amphibrachic quatrain:

> Уж о́н бы с тобо́ю — пола́дил!
> За непринужде́нный покло́н
> Разжа́лованный — Никола́ем,
> Пожа́лованный бы — Петро́м.
>> М. Цветаева, ,,Петр и Пушкин"

The accumulation of these examples in a single stanza
suggests that this is a deliberate device.

Two stresses of this type occur in the poem by J. W.
Paus, on p. 49.

It is clear then that in ternary metres the arrangement
of strong syllables constitutes the permanent framework of

---

[1] Concerning the two hypermetrical stresses in the first anapaest in
Khodasevich's stanza, see p. 52.

the line, unlike the binary metres which tend to preserve the arrangement of their weak syllables.

But there is another difference between ternary and binary metres: whereas in the latter a hypermetrical stress on the first foot of an iambic line is a rare occurrence, ternary metres frequently stress the initial syllables of the amphibrachic and, more especially, of the anapaestic line.

Thus, the word за́втра in the example of the anapaestic line quoted on p. 49 has a hypermetrical stress.

In the following example the two non-metrical stresses render a military command in lines of three-foot anapaestic measure:

> Взво́д вперёд, справа по́-три, не пла́чь!
> Ма́рш моги́льный игра́й, штаб-трубáч!
> А. Фет, „На смерть Бражникова"

Here is another example, of similar measure, in which the hypermetrical stress on всё is caused by an enjambment:

> Задыха́ясь, я кри́кнула: „Шу́тка
> Всё, что бы́ло. Уйдёшь, я умру́".
> Улыбну́лся споко́йно и жу́тко
> И сказа́л мне: „Не сто́й на ветру́".
> А. Ахматова

Pushkin's anapaestic lines normally allow this non-metrical stress. The same applies to half the anapaestic lines in the poetry of Balmont and Blok.[1]

The quotation from Khodasevich on p. 51 contains two hypermetrical stresses, which gives three consecutive stresses on the first foot. This can be the result only of special and altogether exceptional conditions of stress in the line in question:

> Я́, я́, я́. Что за ди́кое сло́во!

A hypermetrical stress on the first foot of an amphi-

---

[1] G. Shengeli, op. cit., p. 66.

brachic line is less common. This gives two consecutive
stresses which emphasize even more distinctly the value
of the first stress. Such a stress occurs on the word он in
Boratynsky's amphibrachic stanza quoted on page 48.
Another example is given below in a four-foot amphibrachic measure:

> Прощай, утешайся, да помни меня.
> Вы, отроки-други, возьмите коня!
>
>   А. Пушкин, „Песнь о вещем Олеге"

In one case only is a breach made in the arrangement of strong syllables. It has been explained above that
the threat of a hiatus of five syllables ensures the preserva-
tion of stress in ternary verse. All the same, this threat does
not hang over the first foot of a dactylic line. In fact, the
removal of the initial stress would produce a sequence of
only three unstressed syllables, which, as has been shown,
is extremely frequent in binary metres. Accordingly, the
first stress in a dactylic line is readily removable under the
same conditions as apply to binary metres. These are:
(1) if a line opens with a word incurring a fourth-syllable
stress; (2) if the first syllable of the line consists of an unstressed word. The following example, composed in four-
foot dactylic measure, combines the two cases:

> Кончились поздно труды роковые.
> Вышли на небо светила ночные,
> И над поверженным лесом луна
> Остановилась, кругла и ясна.
>
>   Н. Некрасов, „Саша"

The stresses are omitted from the first syllables of the
third and fourth lines. In the whole poem, the omission of
the first stress occurs in 11·1 per cent. of lines.

In certain poems the removal of the initial stress is extended and becomes a regular feature of the rhythm. This

happens, for example, in N. S. Gumilev's poem Мужик—
the *moujik* in question is Rasputin—which is written in
three-foot dactylic lines. Here is the opening:

> В го́рдую на́шу столи́цу
> Вхо́дит он — Бо́же, спаси́! —
> Обворожа́ет цари́цу
> Необозри́мой Руси́
>
> Взгля́дом, улы́бкою де́тской,
> Ре́чью тако́й озорно́й, —
> И на груди́ молоде́цкой
> Кре́ст просия́л золото́й.
>
> Как не погну́лись, — о го́ре! —
> Как не поки́нули мест
> Кре́ст на Каза́нском собо́ре
> И на Иса́кии крест?

In six lines out of twelve the initial stress is removed.

In ternary lines, the proportion of accented syllables to
the total number of syllables is 1 to 3. But the presence of
truncated feet at the end of lines, together with hypermetrical accents in the first foot, brings the ratio to something more like 1 to 2·8, which is the proportion in the
spoken language and in binary metres.[1] If, nevertheless,
ternary metres are rarer in Russian than binary, this is not
because of their accentual frequency, which is normal, but
because of the excessively monotonous regularity of the
unstressed intervals, which are invariably disyllabic. In
consequence of this monotony, poets prefer to use iambic
rather than ternary metres in long poems.

Syllabic-accentual versification developed from syllabic
versification in the eighteenth century. The latter, being
based only on a set number of syllables in the line, brought
about an inevitable weakening of stress to prevent it from
degenerating into mere prose. That is why an almost com-

[1] See p. 36.

plete slurring of stress was required in reading syllabic lines aloud. It is quite natural then, that in making stress a part of the system, poets in the syllabic tradition sought to develop first a type of syllabic-accentual line in which stress would play as unimportant a part as possible. The binary verse was unquestionably of this nature. In fact, the facility with which stress disappears in verse of this kind has already been pointed out. That accounts for the preponderance, if not universal employment, of binary metres throughout the eighteenth century and at the same time the delay with which ternary metres found their way into Russian poetry. The impulse given by the syllabic tradition, still so strong in the eighteenth century, made any adjustment of the strong and fixed stress of ternary metres impossible.

There is no question but that poets such as Pushkin or Boratynsky, though marking the beginning of modern verse, in their attitude towards poetry, obviously still look towards the eighteenth century. On the other hand, their younger contemporary, Lermontov, belongs entirely to the nineteenth century. So it is no chance occurrence that there are very few ternary lines in the poetry of the first two, whereas in the poems of Lermontov they abound. Even Zhukovsky has more poems in ternary metres to his credit than Pushkin.

Later, the success of ternary verse was consolidated by its associations with accentual versification, of which the popularity increased in the second half of the nineteenth century.

III

SYLLABIC-ACCENTUAL VERSE:
SECONDARY METRICAL ELEMENTS

THE regular alternation of stressed and unstressed syllables is the basis of syllabic-accentual verse in Russian. It has been shown that the rhythmic application of this principle involves an infinite range of variations, proceeding either from the weakening and disappearance of stress on strong syllables in iambic and trochaic lines, or from the appearance of secondary stresses of varying strength on weak syllables of ternary verse.

This alternation is accompanied by other metrical elements which also produce different rhythmic patterns.

I. THE OPENING OF THE LINE

1. *The first stress in the line*

At the beginning of the line a certain flexibility has been noticed which would be inadmissible within the line. Thus iambic verse may stress the first syllable or replace the first foot with a trochaic foot; trochaic verse may replace the first foot with an iambic foot. In ternary verse, the initial syllable of the first amphibrach or anapaest may take a non-metrical stress; on the other hand, the first dactylic stress can be removed without difficulty.

All these phenomena seem to suggest that, in iambic, trochaic, and dactylic lines, the first accent is in a way outside the rhythmic pattern of the whole. In such verse the pattern acquires its essential value only from the second stress of the line onwards. In amphibrachic and anapaestic lines the accent on the first foot is always present, but even in these it can be preceded, especially in the anapaestic line, by a non-metrical accent.

The accentual variability of the beginning of the line makes it somewhat vague and robs it to some extent of its metrical individuality. This hesitant beginning is in sharp contrast with the end of the line, which is always vigorously emphasized by a stable accent and, above all, by the rhyme.

2. *The anacrusis*

The freedom which the beginning of the line enjoys goes even further. In verse with initial stress—i.e. trochaic or dactylic verse—one or two unstressed syllables may be added before the first stress. This is described by the classical term *anacrusis* (анакру́за). Always unstressed and somewhat outside the body of the line, the anacrusis is less perceptible than an extra syllable inserted before or after the caesura.

Russian makes less use of anacrusis than English or German, in which it is frequent. This is partly due to the treatment given in these languages to the amphibrach, as a dactyl with anacrusis.[1]

Some specimens of anacrusis are found from the eighteenth century onwards, but it is favoured especially by modern poets, and in particular by those who experiment with metre. It is generally limited to ternary metres.

The anacrusis may be used freely, as in the following three-foot dactylic quatrain:

Где́ вы, гряду́щие гу́нны,

Что ту́чей нави́сли над ми́ром?

Слы́шу ваш то́пот чугу́нный

По еще́ не откры́тым Памм́рам.

В. Брюсов, „Грядущие гунны".

---

[1] See p. 45.

This quatrain shows both a one-syllable and a two-syllable anacrusis. The same device is used in the subsequent stanzas, but not always in the same order nor with the same regularity.

Usually, however, anacrusis is a more stable element in the metrical structure of the verse, as in the following lines by A. Fet, composed in three-foot dactylic measure:

Мно́го промча́лось веко́в,	$\unicode{x2013}\unicode{x2013}\|\unicode{x2013}\unicode{x2013}\|\unicode{x2013}$
Сменя́я знамёна и вла́сти,	$\unicode{x2013}\|\unicode{x2013}\unicode{x2013}\|\unicode{x2013}\unicode{x2013}\|\unicode{x2013}\unicode{x2013}$
Мно́го скова́ли око́в	$\unicode{x2013}\unicode{x2013}\|\unicode{x2013}\unicode{x2013}\|\unicode{x2013}$
Вседне́вные ме́лкие стра́сти.	$\unicode{x2013}\|\unicode{x2013}\unicode{x2013}\|\unicode{x2013}\unicode{x2013}\|\unicode{x2013}\unicode{x2013}$

The poem from which this quatrain is taken contains six stanzas in all, and in each of them the second and fourth lines show an anacrusis.

The same poet, A. Fet, has written a poem of two quatrains composed of three-foot dactylic lines in which each odd line shows a disyllabic anacrusis:

То́лько в ми́ре и е́сть, что тени́стый	$\unicode{x2013}\unicode{x2013}\|\unicode{x2013}\unicode{x2013}\|\unicode{x2013}\unicode{x2013}\|\unicode{x2013}\unicode{x2013}$
Дре́млющих клёнов шатёр!	$\unicode{x2013}\unicode{x2013}\|\unicode{x2013}\unicode{x2013}\|\unicode{x2013}$
То́лько в ми́ре и е́сть, что лучи́стый	$\unicode{x2013}\unicode{x2013}\|\unicode{x2013}\unicode{x2013}\|\unicode{x2013}\unicode{x2013}\|\unicode{x2013}\unicode{x2013}$
Де́тски-заду́мчивый взо́р!	$\unicode{x2013}\unicode{x2013}\|\unicode{x2013}\unicode{x2013}\|\unicode{x2013}$

То́лько в ми́ре и е́сть, что души́стый
Ми́лой голо́вки убо́р!
То́лько в ми́ре и е́сть — этот чи́стый,
Вле́во бегу́щий пробо́р!

The device becomes particularly clear because it is always the same word that turns into an anacrusis. Even so, such insistence on this word, repeated four times, almost induces us to place a stress on it. But once stressed, the anacrusis disappears. In such a case this poem would have to be regarded as an exceptionally rare combination

of three anapaests in odd lines, and three dactyls in even
lines, as follows:

$$\acute{}\,\_\,\acute{}\mid\_\,\_\,\acute{}\mid\_\,\_\,\acute{}\mid\_$$
$$\acute{}\,\_\,\_\mid\acute{}\,\_\,\_\mid\acute{}$$

Certain students of Russian verse are inclined to make
the term anacrusis cover every unstressed beginning of a
line. For them, there are only two metres, the trochaic and
the dactylic. The iambic then becomes a trochaic metre,
and the amphibrachic a dactylic metre with a constant
monosyllabic anacrusis, whereas the anapaestic metre
takes the form of a dactylic with a disyllabic anacrusis. In
short, there remains only the contrast between binary and
ternary metres. This point of view scarcely simplifies
things. On the contrary, it tends to standardize the somewhat
different impressions made by the various metres upon us.

II. THE CAESURA

1. *General remarks*

The *caesura* (цезýра) is a pause in the line at a particular
place. It constitutes another of the secondary elements in
the metrical scheme of the line.

In syllabic verse, as has been shown,[1] the caesura is an
essential and obligatory element of the metre. In this type
of verse, therefore, the pause is very marked. Originally,
in Russian syllabic verse, the caesura could be either masculine, when occurring immediately after a stress, or
feminine, when separated from the stress by an unstressed
syllable, with the dactylic, separated from the stress by
two unstressed syllables, as a variant of the masculine
caesura. A characteristic in the development of syllabic
verse in Russia was the gradual disappearance of the feminine caesura. In the poetry of Simeon Polotsky its occurrence varies from 40 to 57 per cent. according to the type

[1] See p. 3.

of poem, whereas in Kantemir's verse it has diminished to 8 per cent., and in his last poems disappeared altogether.[1] In the poem quoted on p. 6, the caesura is masculine in each case.

The syllabic-accentual verse inherited the caesura from the syllabic verse. But in syllabic-accentual verse, with its stresses which indicate the metre distinctly, the caesura is necessarily less important than in purely syllabic verse. In short lines it is not used unless the poet is striving towards a special, and always more or less artificial, effect or convention.

The caesura always coincides with the end of the word, but not necessarily with the end of a foot; it may be placed in the middle of the foot, as for example, in ternary metres. Moreover, it is normally independent of the syntactical break or of a logical pause in the line. The simplest way to remove the caesura is to move the place where the word ends; for the caesura cannot split a word.

In the Russian poetic tradition, it is not necessary for the caesura to come immediately after the stress, as is the case in some syllabic prosodies—in French, for example. In Russian verse, the caesura may occur after trochaic, dactylic, or amphibrachic feet: it may equally well follow an iambic foot whose stress has disappeared. The caesura will be indicated by means of two vertical dashes ||.

2. *The caesura in binary verse*

In iambic and trochaic metres, caesura does not appear in lines of four·feet or less. To introduce it in these lines, a special device is needed, such as the insertion of an extra syllable, or an internal rhyme.[2]

In lines of five feet, the caesura is optional, and when it

[1] L. I. Timofeev, op. cit., p. 129.
[2] See pp. 67, 69.

occurs it is placed after the second foot. A constant caesura
is exceptional in the Russian equivalent of the Shakespearian blank verse,[1] into which it was introduced under
the influence of the French decasyllable. But it is less
monotonous than it is in French verse, since Russian poets
tend to omit the second stress which precedes immediately
the caesura. The constant caesura occurs in Pushkin's
Boris Godunov, of which the opening follows:

> Наряжены́ ‖ мы вме́сте го́род ве́дать,
> Но, ка́жется, ‖ нам не́ за кем смотре́ть:
> Москва́ пуста́; ‖ вослед за патриа́рхом
> К монастырю́ ‖ пошёл и ве́сь наро́д.
> Как ду́маешь, ‖ чем ко́нчится трево́га?

Much more often, however, the caesura is less rigorously
applied, and its frequence oscillates then usually between
70 and 95 per cent.; it practically never falls below 50 per
cent. But a caesura which is not constant can hardly be
called caesura at all. This type of iambic pentameter owes
its origin to the German and English tradition. Zhukovsky
introduced it into Russian poetry by translating Schiller's
Maid of Orleans. It became very frequent and is found, for
example, in *The Little House in Kolomna*, *The Mermaid*, and
the 'little tragedies' by Pushkin, and in the historical
dramas of the nineteenth century by A. K. Tolstoy, Mey,
Ostrovsky, and others. This type of free caesura may be
exemplified by the following extract, taken from *The Stone
Guest* by Pushkin:[2]

> Не пра́вда ли, ‖ он был опи́сан ва́м
> Злоде́ем, и́звергом! О, До́на-Анна!
> Молва́, быть мо́жет, не совсе́м непра́ва;
> На со́вести ‖ уста́лой мно́го зла́,
> Быть мо́жет, тяготе́ет; но с тех по́р,
> Как ва́с уви́дел я, всё измени́лось:
> Мне ка́жется, ‖ я ве́сь перероди́лся!

In lines of six feet and more, the caesura becomes usual if not compulsory, as in the following six-foot iambic lines:

> Пройду́т века́ веко́в, ‖ толпы́ тысячеле́тий,
> Как ту́ча саранчи́, ‖ с собо́й несу́щей сме́рть,
> И в бы́стром ро́поте ‖ испу́ганных столе́тий
> До го́рького конца́ ‖ пребу́дет та́ же твёрдь, —
> Нема́я, мёртвая, ‖ отве́ргнутая Бо́гом,
> Живу́щим далеко́ ‖ в беззвёздных небеса́х,
> В дыха́ньи Ве́чности, ‖ за гра́нью, за поро́гом
> Всего́ поня́тного, ‖ горя́щего в слова́х.
>
> К. Бальмонт

An example of a six-foot trochaic measure with a strongly marked caesura follows:

> Я иду́ доли́ной. ‖ На заты́лке ке́пи.
> В ла́йковой перча́тке ‖ сму́глая рука́.
> Далеко́ сия́ют ‖ ро́зовые сте́пи,
> Широко́ сине́ет ‖ ти́хая ре́ка.
>
> С. Есенин

And here is a rare specimen of an eight-foot trochaic measure:

> На́до ве́чно пе́ть и пла́кать ‖ э́тим стру́нам, зво́нким стру́нам,
> Ве́чно до́лжен би́ться, ви́ться ‖ обезу́мевший смычо́к,
> И под со́лнцем, и под вью́гой, ‖ под беле́ющим буру́ном,
> И когда́ пыла́ет за́пад, ‖ и когда́ гори́т восто́к.
>
> Н. Гумилев, „Волшебная скрипка"

Certain poets with a taste for experiment in versification, such as Fet or Bryusov, sometimes manage to compose entire poems in lines of six or seven feet, without any caesura. Such poems are always feats of exceptional ingenuity.

Folk-poetry makes no use of caesura. Consequently the caesura is excluded from imitations of popular poetry, as, for example, in the six-foot trochaic line examined on page 35.

3. *The caesura in ternary verse*

In ternary verse the caesura usually appears only in lines of four feet or more. Incidentally, longer lines are so exceptional that the question of the caesura in such measures is of no practical interest. It must be stressed that in ternary lines the caesura can easily occur within the foot.

In ternary verse caesura is more marked than in binary verse. In fact, as the stress is constant, the caesura is regularly placed at a set distance from it, whether it appears at the end or in the middle of a foot. This always leads to monotony, though poets try to relieve this effect by avoiding the caesura, in some lines at least.

Here, for example, is the opening of the poem Огородник by Nekrasov, in four-foot anapaestic lines:

> Не гуля́л с кистенём ‖ я в дрему́чем лесу́,
> Не лежа́л я во рву ‖ в непрогля́дную но́чь, —
> Я свой ве́к загуби́л ‖ за деви́цу-красу́,
> За деви́цу-красу́, ‖ за дворя́нскую до́чь.

From the second stanza onwards, though, the author is visibly trying to escape from the monotony of the caesura, which occurs only in the first line:

> Я в неме́цком саду́ ‖ рабо́тал по весне́;
> Во́т, одна́жды, сгреба́ю сучки́ да пою́,
> Гля́дь, — хозя́йская до́чка стои́т в стороне́,
> Смо́трит в о́ба, да слу́шает пе́сню мою́.

In Balmont's poem Безглаго́льность, composed in a four-foot amphibrachic measure, the same intention is noticed, but its achievement is less crude:

> Есть в ру́сской приро́де ‖ уста́лая не́жность,
> Безмо́лвная да́ль затаённой печа́ли,
> Безвы́ходность го́ря, ‖ безгла́сность, безбре́жность.
> Холо́дная вы́сь, уходя́щие да́ли.

Приди́ на рассве́те ‖ на скло́н косого́ра —
Над зы́бкой реко́ю ‖ дыми́тся прохла́да,
Черне́ет грома́да ‖ засты́вшего бо́ра, —
И се́рдцу так бо́льно, ‖ и се́рдце не ра́до.

It follows therefore that in Russian the caesura occurs more rarely in ternary than in binary verse.

4. *The break of the metre at the caesura*

The two hemistichs resulting from the caesura behave, in certain respects, like independent lines. The end of the first hemistich can be extended or reduced, exactly like the end of the line, without reference to the metre of the poem.[1] The beginning of the second hemistich can receive one or two extra syllables, an anacrusis, or can lose a similar number. The result is a breaking of the metre at the caesura that constitutes one of the devices of versification. Needless to say, the caesura is thereby strengthened.

This convention does not appear in Russian until the very end of the eighteenth century. It is found for example, though rarely, in the poetry of Derzhavin. It can be used either occasionally in a single line or throughout the poem as a regular element in the metre. In the diagrams, the syllable left out will be shown by a °, and the syllable added by a plus sign.

Here is an example of a poem composed in four-foot dactylic measure, with the caesura occurring after the second syllable of the second foot:

Мно́го земе́ль я ‖ оста́вил за мно́ю;
Вы́нес я мно́го ‖ смяте́нной душо́ю
Ра́достей ло́жных, ‖ и́стинных зо́л;
Мно́го мятѐжных ‖ реши́л я вопро́сов,
Пре́жде чем ру́ки ‖ Марсе́льских матро́сов
По́дняли я́корь, ‖ наде́жды симво́л!

Е. Боратынский, „Пироскаф“

[1] See p. 13.

$$\acute{-} -- \mid \acute{-} - \mid\mid - \mid \acute{-} -- \mid \acute{-} -$$
$$\acute{-} -- \mid \acute{-} - \mid\mid - \mid \acute{-} -- \mid \acute{-} -$$
$$\acute{-} -- \mid \acute{-} - \mid\mid \circ \mid \acute{-} -- \mid \acute{-}$$
$$\acute{-} -- \mid \acute{-} - \mid\mid - \mid \acute{-} -- \mid \acute{-} -$$
$$\acute{-} -- \mid \acute{-} - \mid\mid - \mid \acute{-} -- \mid \acute{-} -$$
$$\acute{-} -- \mid \acute{-} - \mid\mid - \mid \acute{-} -- \mid \acute{-}$$

One syllable is omitted at the beginning of the second
hemistich in the third line. In this poem, which has in all
six stanzas, one syllable is omitted once in four stanzas and
twice in one stanza. Clearly the occurrence of this convention here is simply a remote accident.

Its occurrence becomes more systematic in the following
poem, written in 1800, in the same metre, with a similar
caesura. The poem is one of the earliest to use this convention:

Кто́ перед ра́тью ‖ бу́дет, пыла́я,	$\acute{-} -- \mid \acute{-} - \mid\mid \circ \mid \acute{-} -- \mid \acute{-} -$
Е́здить на кля́че, ‖ е́сть сухари́;	$\acute{-} -- \mid \acute{-} - \mid\mid \circ \mid \acute{-} -- \mid \acute{-}$
В сту́же и в зно́е ‖ ме́ч закаля́я,	$\acute{-} -- \mid \acute{-} - \mid\mid \circ \mid \acute{-} -- \mid \acute{-} -$
Спа́ть на соло́ме, ‖ бде́ть до зари́,	$\acute{-} -- \mid \acute{-} - \mid\mid \circ \mid \acute{-} -- \mid \acute{-}$
Ты́сячи во́инств, ‖ сте́н и затво́ров,	$\acute{-} -- \mid \acute{-} - \mid\mid \circ \mid \acute{-} -- \mid \acute{-} -$
С го́рстью Россия́н ‖ всё́ побежда́ть?	$\acute{-} -- \mid \acute{-} - \mid\mid \circ \mid \acute{-} -- \mid \acute{-}$

Г. Держа́вин, „Снигирь“

In this stanza, it may be added, there is nothing to prevent
the placing of the caesura *after* the syllable omitted
($\acute{-} -- \mid \acute{-} - \circ \mid\mid \acute{-} -- \mid \acute{-} -$). Out of the twenty-four lines composing this poem, only one appears complete:

По́лно петь пе́сню ‖ вое́нну, снигирь!
$$\acute{-} -- \mid \acute{-} - \mid\mid - \mid \acute{-} -- \mid \acute{-}$$

On account of this line it is correct to place the caesura in
the middle of the second foot, as has been shown in the
example.

A caesura of the same type is found in imitation of the
elegiac couplet of classical poetry. In Greek and Latin verse,
the couplet is the combination of a hexameter, an odd line,

with a pentameter,[1] an even line. In the Russian imitation, which is more immediately inspired by German models than by the classical original, the odd line is a six-foot dactylic, consisting of seventeen syllables, with a weak caesura inside the third foot and a trochaic ending, and the even line too is a six-foot dactylic, consisting of fourteen syllables, in which two syllables are omitted at the caesura and the last foot is reduced to one stressed syllable. The caesura acquires added strength in the even line, because it is placed between two successive stresses, and the break in the metre is extremely sharp:

> Смéртный, гони́мый людьми́ ‖ и судьбóй! расставáяся с ми́ром,
> Злóбу людéй и судьбы́ ‖ сéрдцем прости́ и забýдь.
> К сóлнцу впослéднее взóр ‖ обрати́, как Руссó, и утéшься:
> В тéрнах заснýвшие здéсь, ‖ в ми́ртах пробýдятся тáм.
>
> А. Дéльвиг, „Утешение"

```
‿ – – | ‿ – – | ‿ ‖ – – | ‿ – – | ‿ – – | ‿ –
‿ – – | ‿ ⊤ – | ‿ ‖ ○ ○ | ‿ – – | ‿ – – | ‿
‿ – – | ‿ – – | ‿ ‖ – – | ‿ – – | ‿ – – | ‿ –
‿ – – | ‿ – – | ‿ ‖ ○ ○ | ‿ – – | ‿ – – | ‿
```

The even line is cut by the caesura into two completely equal hemistichs, as it is also in this excellent translation of an elegiac couplet by Schiller,[2] in which the break in the metre harmonizes perfectly with the image evoked:

> Бьёт во гекзáметре ввéрх ‖ водянáя колóнна фонтáна,
> Чтóбы в пентáметре внóвь ‖ мéрно, певýче упáсть.

The caesura reinforced by an extra syllable has been widely exploited by the symbolist poets and their fol-

---

[1] This line is in fact a hexameter of which the third and the sixth feet are catalectic.

[2] Here is the text of the German original, composed in a less rigorous measure:

> Im Hexameter steigt ‖ des Springquells flüssige Säule,
> Im Pentameter drauf ‖ fällt sie melodisch herab.

lowers, notably by Balmont, who made it a permanent feature of his versification. Here is an extract from one of his poems composed in four-foot anapaestic lines, in which every even line includes an extra syllable before the caesura:

> Я мечтóю ловѝл ‖ уходя́щие тѐни,
> Уходя́щие тѐни ‖ погасáвшего дня́.
> Я на бáшню всходѝл, ‖ и дрожáли ступѐни,
> И дрожáли ступѐни ‖ под ногóй у меня́.

```
─ ─ ´ | ─ ─ ´ |       ‖ ─ ─ ´ | ─ ─ ´ | ─
─ ─ ´ | ─ ─ ´ | + ‖ ─ ─ ´ | ─ ─ ´
─ ─ ´ | ─ ─ ´ |       ‖ ─ ─ ´ | ─ ─ ´ | ─
─ ─ ´ | ─ ─ ´ | + ‖ ─ ─ ´ | ─ ─ ´
```

Syntactical devices, the repetition of the second hemistich at the beginning of the following line and a parallel between the first hemistichs of the odd lines, emphasize still further the importance of the caesura in this poem.

A similar use of the caesura will be found in Igor Severyanin's poem quoted on page 151.

In the poem Нелюбовь by Z. Hippius, written in four-foot iambic lines, an extra syllable at the caesura is inserted in all sixteen lines of the four stanzas. Indeed, it is precisely this extra syllable placed after the second foot and at the end of a word which occasions the caesura. The first stanza of this poem follows, in the odd lines of which the two hemistichs are absolutely equal:

> Как вéтер мóкрый ‖ — ты бьёшься в стáвни,
> Как вéтер чёрный ‖ поёшь: ты мóй!
> Я дрéвний хáос, ‖ я дрýг твой дáвний,
> Твой дрýг едѝный, ‖ — открóй, открóй!

```
─ ´ | ─ ´ | + ‖ ─ ´ | ─ ´ | ─
─ ´ | ─ ´ | + ‖ ─ ´ | ─ ´
─ ´ | ─ ´ | + ‖ ─ ´ | ─ ´ | ─
─ ´ | ─ ´ | + ‖ ─ ´ | ─ ´
```

This quatrain is also a rare example of the complete application of the metrical scheme, with its four stresses in each line.

The following poem by F. Sologub, written in eight-foot iambics, presents an abundance of caesuras with supplementary syllables:

На све́те мно́го | благоуха́нной ‖ и озарённой красоты́.
Заба́ва де́вам, | отра́да же́нам ‖ — весе́нне-бе́лые цветы́.
Цвето́в весе́нних | миле́е же́ны, ‖ жела́нней де́вы | — о ни́х мечты́.
Но кто́ изве́дал | укло́ны жи́зни ‖ до ве́чно-тёмной, | ночно́й черты́,
Кто ви́дел ру́ку | над колыбе́лью ‖ у надмоги́льной, | немо́й плиты́,
Тому́ поня́тно, | что в бе́дном се́рдце ‖ печа́ль и ра́дость | наве́к слиты́.
Лику́й и сме́йся | над ве́щей бе́здной, ‖ всходи́ беспе́чно | на все́ мосты́,
А эти сто́ны: | — Дыша́ть мне не́чем, ‖ я умира́ю! | — поймёшь ли ты́?

```
– ́ | – ́ | + ‖ – – | – ́ | + ‖‖ – – | – ́ | – – | – ́
– ́ | – ́ | + ‖ – ́ | – ́ | + ‖‖ – ́ | – ́ | – – | – ́
– ́ | – ́ | + ‖ – ́ | – ́ | + ‖‖ – ́ | – ́ | + ‖ – ́ | · – ́
– ́ | – ́ | + ‖ – ́ | – ́ | + ‖‖ – ́ | – ́ | + ‖ – ́ | – ́
– ́ | – ́ | + ‖ – – | – ́ | + ‖‖ – – | – ́ | + ‖ – ́ | – ́
– ́ | – ́ | + ‖ – ́ | – ́ | + ‖‖ – ́ | – ́ | + ‖ – ́ | – ́
– ́ | – ́ | + ‖ – ́ | – ́ | + ‖‖ – ́ | – ́ | + ‖ – ́ | – ́
– – | – ́ | + ‖ – ́ | – ́ | + ‖‖ – – | – ́ | + ‖ – ́ | – ́
```

The line is cut in two by a strong caesura which is preceded by an extra syllable. From the third line onwards, each hemistich contains a caesura of the same kind. Thus the line is made up of four sections, the first three of which are identical in structure. These consist of five syllables forming two iambic feet with a trochaic clausula. The fourth section comprises two iambic feet with a masculine rhyme. The stresses are applied regularly. The extra syllables at the caesura give a lilt to the line. In the first two lines the second hemistich has no extra syllables after the second foot, and, without these, contains no caesura.

Finally, it is a distinction of the poem that it employs the same rhyme, ты, throughout.

5. *Internal rhyme*

One effective way of strengthening the caesura is by the use of internal rhyme, which means that two hemistichs of the same line, or the first hemistichs of two successive lines, are rhymed. Internal rhyme can take place only at the caesura, otherwise it remains inoperative, or, worse still, conveys the impression of a phonetic accident which may tend to diminish the aesthetic value of the line.

Two stanzas follow from a poem in a four-foot trochaic metre with an abundance of internal rhymes, which uses both the conventions mentioned above. A binary line of four feet generally has no caesura: this is supplied by the internal rhyme. The first quatrain is a rare example of the complete application of the four metrical stresses:

> Ря́ны кра́ски. ‖ Во́здух чи́ст.
> Вьётся в пля́ске ‖ кра́сный ли́ст.
> Э́то о́сень, ‖ да́лей про́синь,
> Гу́лы со́сен, ‖ ве́ток сви́ст.
>
> Ве́тер кло́нит ‖ ря́д раки́т,
> Ли́стья го́нит ‖ и вихри́т
> Ви́хрей ра́ти, ‖ а на ска́те
> Переката́ти ‖ - по́ле мчи́т.
>
>   М. Волошин, „Осень"

It will be noticed that in the last line the caesura is particularly effective, since it cuts a compound word into two: перекати́-по́ле, the name of a plant (*Gypsophila paniculata*) which the wind uproots, forms into a ball, and sends rolling across the fields, whence its name. The originality of this caesura is further emphasized by the shift in the stress that it demands: перека́ти-по́ле.

Internal rhyme can be combined with a break in the rhythm at the caesura, as has been shown in the previous section. Here is an example, taken from a ballad adapted by Pushkin from Mickiewicz. Composed in a measure of alternate four-foot and three-foot anapaestic lines, the ballad introduces an extra syllable at the caesura:

> Три у Бу́дрыса сы́на, как и о́н три литви́на,
> Он пришёл толкова́ть с молодца́ми.
> „Де́ти! Се́дла чини́те, лошаде́й проводи́те,
> Да точи́те мечи́ с бердыша́ми".

$$- - \acute{-} \mid - - \acute{-} \mid + \parallel - - \acute{-} \mid - - \acute{-} \mid -$$
$$- - \acute{-} \mid - - \acute{-} \mid - - \acute{-} \mid -$$
$$\acute{-} - \acute{-} \mid - - \acute{-} \mid + \parallel - - \acute{-} \mid - - \acute{-} \mid -$$
$$- - \acute{-} \mid - - \acute{-} \mid - - \acute{-} \mid -$$

The third line has a stress on the first syllable, a common occurrence in anapaestic lines. It is obvious that the extra syllable at the caesura cuts the line into two absolutely equal hemistichs, consisting of two anapaestic feet with feminine rhyme. Internal rhyme gives them complete autonomy. Incidentally, there is nothing to prevent these hemistichs being regarded as independent lines and the quatrain as a tail-rhyme stanza of six lines (of $2+2+3+2+2+3$ anapaestic feet):

> Три у Бу́дрыса сы́на,
> Как и о́н три литви́на,
> Он пришёл толкова́ть с молодца́ми.
> „Де́ти! Се́дла чини́те,
> Лошаде́й проводи́те,
> Да точи́те мечи́ с бердыша́ми!"

When internal rhyme is applied systematically in a poem, it normally cuts the line into two independent parts. That is exactly what happens in the two examples quoted. In other words, too often internal rhyme is only the result of a purely typographical arrangement of the lines, which emphasizes the fact that there is no very clear distinction between the conception of the line and that of the hemistich.

It has been pointed out already that to use internal rhyme where there is no caesura is merely to beat the air. The following four-foot trochaic quatrain of Bryusov effectively proves this. To distinguish the internal rhymes, the lines are set out in two columns:

Детских плеч	твоих дрожанье,
Детских глаз	недоуменье,
Миги встреч,	часы свиданья,
Долгий час,	как век томленья.

When reciting this stanza the internal rhymes may escape notice altogether, and their typographical spacing serves to emphasize their sterile quality.

III. THE END OF THE LINE

More peculiarities affect the end than the beginning of the line.

Some of these have been mentioned already, for example, the compulsory stress on the last foot in binary metres,[1] and the special treatment of the final foot which can be either truncated by one or two weak syllables, or lengthened by several unstressed syllables.[2] Also, the regular sequence of strong and weak syllables ends with the last stress of the line, and unstressed syllables following this stress do not add to the number of feet.

Rhyme is the most important characteristic of the end of the line. But, since it is common to all types of versification, it will be examined in detail in Chapter VI, at the end of the study. Purely rhythmic elements, as, for example, enjambment, will be dealt with in Chapter V.

[1] See p. 17.   [2] See p. 13.

IV. THE NUMBER OF FEET IN THE LINE

The number of feet in a line of Russian poetry naturally varies. The following numbers are the most frequent: four in binary metres—from seven to ten syllables; three in ternary metres—from seven to eleven syllables. In this respect Russian scarcely differs from English and German.

Needless to say, there are many shorter, as well as many longer, lines, as the examples clearly show. Longer lines have a tendency to split up into hemistichs, in other words, the caesura comes in. If the hemistichs themselves become too long, if they exceed four feet in binary verse and three feet in ternary verse, the unity of the line is completely broken, and each hemistich becomes a line on its own.

The number of feet may remain constant in each line, but even so there is a difference in the number of syllables in the last 'foot and beyond it, which makes possible the variation of masculine, feminine, and dactylic rhyming.

Often, though, the number of feet varies from one line to another. Two examples of this may be given:

1. When no principle dictates the number of feet, the poet can dispose of lines of irregular lengths according to his semantic and syntactical needs: i.e. in *free verse* (вóльный стих). The favourite poetic form for free verse is the fable,[1] but from time to time it is found in other forms of poetry. There again, the practice of Russian hardly differs from that of English and German and even resembles French practice. But since free verse is based on no given scheme, there is no reason to examine it in a chapter devoted to the *metrical* elements of verse. It will be dealt with in more detail in Chapter V, which is concerned with the rhythmic elements of poetry.

[1] See p. 121.

2. It may happen that variations in the number of feet are repeated regularly according to a scheme which the poet has imposed on himself, so that they constitute a metrical element in a line. Practically the only occurrence of this is in poems divided into stanzas. It is therefore more logical to treat such variants as belonging to the stanza form which will be examined in the following section.

V. THE STANZA

The grouping of lines in *stanzas* (строфá) has been usual in Russian poetry ever since the syllabic period. Even so, in this type of poetry, the stanza has played a very minor role, not entirely to be explained by the monotony of the rhyme, which was always feminine. In the work of Simeon Polotsky, for example, each poem forms a metrical whole which, more often than not, cannot be divided into stanzas.

The idea of the stanza, in the modern sense of the word, evolves with the triumph of syllabic-accentual poetry. In his treatise of 1752 Trediakovsky gives seventeen examples of stanzas, both iambic and trochaic, containing from four to ten lines.

In Russian syllabic-accentual poetry, three elements combine to form the stanza: (1) the number of lines in the stanza, (2) the alternation of rhymes, and (3) the number of feet in a line.

In accentual poetry, the third element, which seems essential, has no place, and reduced to the two first elements, the stanza plays a less important role. Both by its nature and its history, the conception of the stanza belongs to the syllabic-accentual tradition and that is why it is examined here, among the secondary elements of the metre.

In none of the three elements of the stanza does Russian show peculiarities which do not exist in other European systems of versification. In this respect, stanza form in Russian shows very little originality, being for the most part borrowed.

Regarding the number of lines in the stanza, a minimum of four is necessary: that is the normal requirement of Western European poetry. The maximum is not fixed by rule. Nevertheless, if a stanza has to retain its metrical integrity, from an acoustic point of view, this maximum must not be too high. Certainly the maximum seems to have been reached in the fourteen-line stanza of *Evgeny Onegin*.

The alternation of rhymes is left entirely to the discretion of the poet. In a four-line stanza, the most usual arrangement is that of alternate rhymes *a b a b*. In longer stanzas it is usual to vary the combinations and to join rhyming couplets, *c c*, to alternate rhymes as well as enclosing rhymes *d e e d*. A triplet, or three lines rhyming together, is relatively rare: when it does occur it is usually embraced by enclosing rhyme, *a b b b a*. For an enclosing rhyme a gap of three lines is the limit beyond which it becomes impossible to recall the rhyme.[1] The examples are supplied in subsections 1–3.

As for the number of feet in the line, this number may be either constant or variable.

1. *The stanza composed of lines with a constant number of feet*

In a stanza the number of the feet may be constant in every line, but the number of syllables may vary in accordance with the alternation of different kinds of rhyme. The simplest and also by far the most frequent stanza form in Russian poetry is a quatrain consisting of four-foot

---

[1] Concerning the use of rhyme, see Chapter VI.

iambics, with alternate feminine and masculine rhymes, for example:

   a Всё, что минýтно, всё, что брéнно,
   b Похоронúла ты в векáх.
   a Ты́, как младéнец, спúшь, Равéнна,
   b У сóнной вéчности в рукáх.

                             А. Блок, ,,Равенна"

The substitution of the trochee for the iambus will be noted in the first feet of the odd lines.

Enclosing rhymes, but not rhyming couplets, are equally possible, though less frequent, in this form of stanza. By using the masculine, feminine, and dactylic rhyming and by varying the combinations, twelve variants of this stanza may be achieved. The same applies to any four-line stanza composed of lines with a fixed number of feet. Every increase of the number of lines in a stanza increases also the number of rhyme combinations. Clearly it is impossible to review them all, and a few examples only will be given of the better-known forms of stanza.

In the five-line stanza the problem is how to add the fifth line to the quatrain. Ordinarily it is placed either after the third line, making the rhyme-scheme *a b a a b*, or after the fourth, producing *a b a b a*. Other combinations are possible, though they are seldom used. Here is an example of the first type, composed of four-foot trochaic lines:

   a Громоздя́ на стéны стéны,
   b Рýшишь ты за вáлом вáл.
   a Но всегдá страшáсь измéны,
   a Покрывáлом бéлой пéны
   b Крóешь плéчи смýглых скáл.

                         В. Брюсов, ,,Над океаном"

The six-line stanza is usually built on three rhymes. Either a quatrain of alternate rhymes is preceded or followed by a rhyming couplet, forming *a a b c b c*, or *a b a b c c*, or a rhyming couplet precedes a quatrain with enclosing rhymes in what is described as a *tail-rhyme stanza*: *a a b c c b*. But it can also be constituted simply with alternate rhymes: *a b a b a b*. An iambic tail-rhyme stanza of four-foot lines follows:

a   Я те́ло в кре́сло уроню́,

a   Я све́т рука́ми заслоню́,

b   И бу́ду пла́кать до́лго, до́лго,

c   Припомина́я вечера́,

c   Когда не му́чило „вчера́"

b   И не томи́ли це́пи до́лга.

Н. Гумилев

An amphibrachic stanza of the first type by Boratynsky is quoted on p. 48, and 'The Song of the President' from *The Feast at the Time of Plague*, an adaptation by Pushkin of John Wilson's *The City of the Plague*, is composed with a similar rhyme-scheme.

The eight-line stanza shows a great variety of combinations, the least interesting of which is the juxtaposition of two quatrains of alternate rhymes. An example of an eight-line stanza is given, in six-foot iambic lines, with a caesura after the third foot:

a   Уны́лая пора́, ‖ оче́й очарова́нье,

b   Прия́тна мне твоя́ ‖ проща́льная краса́ —

a   Люблю́ я пы́шное ‖ приро́ды увяда́нье,

b   В багре́ц и зо́лото ‖ оде́тые леса́ —

a   В их се́нях ве́тра шум ‖ и све́жее дыха́нье,

b   И мгло́й волни́стою ‖ покры́ты небеса́,

c   И ре́дкий со́лнца луч, ‖ и пе́рвые моро́зы,

c   И отдалённые ‖ седо́й Зимы́ угро́зы.

А. Пушкин, „Осень"

The above type of stanza, though in five-foot iambics, was used for the first time by Zhukovsky in an elegy on the death of the Queen of Württemberg. It was then used by Pushkin in *The Little House in Kolomna*. This is the Russian equivalent of the *ottava rima* or *octave* of Italian and Spanish poetry which Zhukovsky had imported into Russia. It is also the stanza of Byron's *Don Juan*.

The ten-line stanza of four-foot iambic lines was in the eighteenth century the stanza selected for the most distinguished poetic form, the ode. An example follows:

a   Идут в молчании глубоком,
b   Во мрачной, страшной тишине,
a   Собой пренебрегают, роком;
b   Зарница только в вышине
c   По их оружию играет,
c   И только их душа сияет,
d   Когда на бой, на смерть идёт.
e   Уж блещут молнии крылами,
e   Уж осыпаются громами;
d   Они молчат, идут вперёд.

Г. Державин, „На взятие Измаила"

This stanza is shown to be a combination of a quatrain with alternate rhymes and of a tail-rhyme stanza.[1] It is also found in Western European poetry.[2]

There is no point in adding indefinitely to the examples quoted, but because of its importance, attention must be drawn to the stanza-form in *Evgeny Onegin*, which contains fourteen four-foot iambic lines and rhymes *a b a b c c d d e f f e g g*:

a   Любви все возрасты покорны;
b   Но юным, девственным сердцам
a   Её порывы благотворны,
b   Как бури вешние полям.
c   В дожде страстей они свежеют,
c   И обновляются, и зреют —
d   И жизнь могущая даёт
d   И пышный цвет, и сладкий плод.

[1] Another example of this stanza, in an ode by Lomonosov, is given on p. 21.

[2] For example, in the ode *An sein Vaterland*, by J. Ch. Günther, a poet from whom Lomonosov borrowed certain metrical forms.

e Но в во́зраст по́здний и беспло́дный,
f   На поворо́те на́ших ле́т,
f   Печа́лен стра́сти ме́ртвый сле́д;
e Так бу́ри о́сени холо́дной
g В боло́то обраща́ют лу́г
g И обнажа́ют ле́с вокру́г.

viii. 29

This is also a combination of a quatrain and a tail-rhyme stanza, though in this example each is supplemented by a couplet.

2. *The stanza composed of lines with a variable number of feet*

Stanzas composed of lines with a variable number of feet are in no way different from those in the preceding category, as far as the arrangement of lines is concerned. Accordingly, this section will be confined to a consideration of the relative length of the line. But, from the infinite variety of stanza combinations, a few examples only are possible.

The most frequent example is that in which certain lines, usually even, and less often odd, lose a foot in relation to others. Here is a stanza combining trochaic lines of four and three feet:

a Шо́пот. Ро́бкое дыха́нье.   ´– | ´– | –– | ´–
b   Тре́ли соловья́.   ´– | –– | ´
a Серебро́ и колыха́нье   –– | ´– | –– | ´–
b   Со́нного ручья́.   ´– | –– | ´

А. Фет

Between odd lines and even lines with the last foot cut off, there is a difference of three syllables. It should be noted, in passing, that this famous poem contains no verb, nor indeed any predicate, in all of its three stanzas.

In the following eight-line stanza, which is taken from Pushkin's poem *The Bridegroom*, the rhythmic effect is a

specially successful one, and the difference between
the lines of four- and three-foot iambics is reduced to one
syllable:

a	Три дня́ купе́ческая до́чь	$- \underset{\cdot}{\prime} \mid - \underset{\cdot}{\prime} \mid - - \mid - \underset{\cdot}{\prime}$
b	Ната́ша пропада́ла;	$- \underset{\cdot}{\prime} \mid - - \mid - \underset{\cdot}{\prime} \mid -$
a	Она́ во дво́р на тре́тью но́чь	$- - \mid - \underset{\cdot}{\prime} \mid - \underset{\cdot}{\prime} \mid - \underset{\cdot}{\prime}$
b	Без па́мяти вбежа́ла.	$- \underset{\cdot}{\prime} \mid - - \mid - \underset{\cdot}{\prime} \mid -$
c	С вопро́сами оте́ц и ма́ть	$- \underset{\cdot}{\prime} \mid - - \mid - \underset{\cdot}{\prime} \mid - \underset{\cdot}{\prime}$
c	К Ната́ше ста́ли приступа́ть.	$- \underset{\cdot}{\prime} \mid - \underset{\cdot}{\prime} \mid - - \mid - \underset{\cdot}{\prime}$
d	Ната́ша их не слы́шит,	$- \underset{\cdot}{\prime} \mid - - \mid - \underset{\cdot}{\prime} \mid -$
d	Дрожи́т и еле ды́шит.	$- \underset{\cdot}{\prime} \mid - - \mid - \underset{\cdot}{\prime} \mid -$

Other examples are the trochaic stanza of Zhukovsky
built up on alternating lines of four and three feet,[1] and
the iambic hymn of Pastor Glück.[2]

An uneven number of feet does not necessarily lead to
an uneven number of syllables. In fact, if, in an iambic
poem, the four-foot line contains a masculine rhyme,
while the three-foot line has a dactylic rhyme, the two
lines will have the same syllabic length, as is shown in the
following quatrain:

a	О, говори́ хоть ты́ со мно́й,	$- - \mid - \underset{\cdot}{\prime} \mid - \underset{\cdot}{\prime} \mid - \underset{\cdot}{\prime}$
b	Подру́га семистру́нная!	$- \underset{\cdot}{\prime} \mid - - \mid - \underset{\cdot}{\prime} \mid - -$
a	Душа́ полна́ тако́й тоско́й,	$- \underset{\cdot}{\prime} \mid - \underset{\cdot}{\prime} \mid - \underset{\cdot}{\prime} \mid - \underset{\cdot}{\prime}$
b	А но́чь така́я лу́нная!	$- \underset{\cdot}{\prime} \mid - \underset{\cdot}{\prime} \mid - \underset{\cdot}{\prime} \mid - -$

А. Григо́рьев

This poem is especially known as a romance.

The same principle, but with a different distribution of
rhymes, may lead to lines which vary considerably in
length, as in the following stanza of seven lines, written in
four- and three-foot iambic lines:

a	Скажи́-ка, дя́дя, ведь неда́ром,	$- \underset{\cdot}{\prime} \mid - \underset{\cdot}{\prime} \mid - - \mid - \underset{\cdot}{\prime} \mid -$
a	Москва́, спалённая пожа́ром,	$- \underset{\cdot}{\prime} \mid - \underset{\cdot}{\prime} \mid - - \mid - \underset{\cdot}{\prime} \mid -$
b	Францу́зу отдана́?	$- \underset{\cdot}{\prime} \mid - - \mid - \underset{\cdot}{\prime}$

---

[1] See p. 31.   [2] See p. 22.

c	Ведь бы́ли ж схва́тки боевы́е!	– ´ | – ´ | – – | – ´ | –
c	Да говоря́т, ещё каки́е!	– – | – ´ | – – | – ´ | –
c	Неда́ром по́мнит вся Росси́я	– ´ | – ´ | – ´ | – ´ | –
b	Про де́нь Бородина́!	– ´ | – – | – ´

М. Ле́рмонтов, „Бородино́"

In this poem the reader will observe an example of a triplet, a formula of rhyme that is infrequent.

Infinite variety is possible in the stanza-form by using
lines of different lengths. One can imagine, for example, a
progressive decrease of feet in successive lines, as in the
following iambic stanza of 5+5+4+3 feet:

a	Заду́мчивый, он ча́сто по кладби́щу
b	При скло́не дня́ ходи́л среди кресто́в:
a	Его́ тоске́ дава́ло пи́щу
b	Споко́йствие гробо́в.

В. Жуко́вский, „Эльвина и Эдвин"

– ´ \| – – \| – ´ \| – – \| – ´ \| –
– ´ \| – ´ \| – ´ \| – – \| – ´
– – \| – ´ \| – ´ \| – ´ \| –
– ´ \| – – \| – ´

Or again, in this iambic stanza of eight lines of
5+4+2+4+5+4+2+5 feet and with two triplets:

a	Марки́з гуля́ет с дру́гом в цветнике́,
a	У ка́ждого левко́й в руке́,
a	А в парнике́
b	Сквозь стёкла ви́дны анана́сы.
c	Веду́т они инти́мный разгово́р,
c	С улы́бкой взор встреча́ет взор,
c	Цветно́й узо́р
b	Пестри́т жиле́тов не́жные атла́сы.

М. Кузми́н, „Разгово́р"

– ´ \| – ´ \| – ´ \| – – \| – ´
– ´ \| – – \| – ´ \| – ´
– – \| – ´
– ´ \| – ´ \| – – \| – ´ \| –

$$- \acute{\;} \,|\, - - \,|\, - \acute{\;} \,|\, - - \,|\, - \acute{\;}$$
$$- \acute{\;} \,|\, - \acute{\;} \,|\, - \acute{\;} \,|\, - \acute{\;}$$
$$- \acute{\;} \,|\, - \acute{\;}$$
$$- \acute{\;} \,|\, - \acute{\;} \,|\, - \acute{\;} \,|\, - - \,|\, - \acute{\;} \,|\, -$$

The metrical pattern of a stanza may be capricious and the difference in the length of the lines considerable, as in the following stanza which contains alternate rhymes of five-foot and two-foot iambics, making a difference of seven syllables between adjacent lines:

a	Что красоты́, ‖ почти всегда́ лука́вой,
b	Мне до́лгий взо́р!
a	Обма́нчив о́н! ‖ знако́м с его отра́вой
b	Я с да́вних по́р.
c	Обма́нчив о́н! ‖ Его жива́я сла́дость
d	Душе́ мое́й
c	Страшна́ тепе́рь! ‖ Что пре́жде было в ра́дость,
d	То в му́ку е́й.

Е. Боратынский

$$\acute{\;} - \,|\, - \acute{\;} \,\|\, - - \,|\, - \acute{\;} \,|\, - \acute{\;} \,|\, -$$
$$- \acute{\;} \,|\, - \acute{\;}$$
$$- \acute{\;} \,|\, - \acute{\;} \,\|\, - \acute{\;} \,|\, - - \,|\, - \acute{\;} \,|\, -$$
$$- \acute{\;} \,|\, - \acute{\;}$$
$$- \acute{\;} \,|\, - \acute{\;} \,\|\, - - \,|\, - \acute{\;} \,|\, - \acute{\;} \,|\, -$$
$$- \acute{\;} \,|\, - \acute{\;}$$
$$- \acute{\;} \,|\, - \acute{\;} \,\|\, - \acute{\;} \,|\, - - \,|\, - \acute{\;} \,|\, -$$
$$- \acute{\;} \,|\, - \acute{\;}$$

A trochee in place of an iambus will be observed in the first foot of the first line. Also worth noting is the possibility of the full development of the rhythm in the metrical scheme, on condition that the numerous words with ambiguous accentuation are stressed. Examples are: почти́, еró (twice), and бы́ло.

The following stanza is a rather elaborate combination of amphibrachic lines of two and four feet:

a	На тёмные сво́ды
b	Багря́ным щито́м покати́лась луна́;

<pre>
a   И о́зера во́ды
b   Струи́стым сия́ньем покры́ла она́;
c   От за́мка, от се́ней
d   Дубра́в по брега́м
c   Огро́мные те́ней
d   Легли́ велика́ны по гла́дким волна́м.
</pre>

В. Жуковский „Эолова арфа"

<pre>
_ ´ _ | _ ´ _
_ ´ _ | _ ´ _ | _ ´ _ | _ ´
_ ´ _ | _ ´ _
_ ´ _ | _ ´ _ | _ ´ _ | _ ´
_ ´ _ | _ ´ _
_ ´ _ | _ ´
_ ´ _ | _ ´ _
_ ´ _ | _ ´ _ | _ ´ _ | _ ´
</pre>

In many of his poems which are translations or adaptations of foreign originals, Zhukovsky simply imitated the stanza form of his model, but frequently in other poems he altered the verse structure.

Finally, stanzas may be envisaged which are composed of lines of different metres. Examples of this are extremely rare. Here is one taken from A. K. Tolstoy, who was highly skilled in the art of verse composition. It shows a combination of four-foot anapaestic lines alternating with a one-foot trochaic line placed in enjambment:

<pre>
a a   У прика́зных воро́т ǁ собира́лся наро́д
  b   Гу́сто;
c c   Говори́л в простоте́, ǁ что в его́ животе́
  b   Пу́сто.
d d   Дурачьё! сказал дья́к, ǁ из вас до́лжен быть вся́к
  e   В те́ле:
f f   Ещё в ду́ме вчера́ ǁ мы с трудо́м осетра́
  e   Съе́ли.
</pre>

<pre>
_ _ ´ | _ _ ´ ǁ _ _ ´ | _ _ ´
´ _
_ _ ´ | _ _ ´ ǁ _ _ ´ | _ _ ´
´ _
</pre>

The extreme unevenness of the lines serves to intensify the fanciful nature of this device. But since there is an internal rhyme at the caesura, it is perfectly in order to regard this stanza as a combination of two two-foot anapaestic lines and a one-foot trochaic line repeated four times. In this example perhaps it is more readily conceivable as two stanzas of six lines, i.e. two tail-rhyme stanzas.

Sometimes the anacrusis may give the impression of a combination of different metres.[1]

3. *Poems in set form*

Of set forms of poetry, which were imported, only the sonnet (сонет) was adopted definitively in Russian poetry and that has been retained into modern times. In the Russian sonnet the stanza-structure is strictly observed. It consists of two quatrains employing alternate rhymes, followed by a six-line stanza, divided into two tercets and using three rhymes, in which a rhyming couplet is followed by two alternate rhymes. The six-line stanza can also be a tail-rhyme stanza. The metre is the five-foot iambic line:

a	Суровый Дант не презирал сонета;
b	В нём жар любви Петрарка изливал;
a	Игру его любил творец Макбета;
b	Им скорбну мысль Камоэнс облскал.
a	И в наши дни пленяет он поэта;
b	Вордсворт его орудием избрал,
a	Когда, вдали от суетного света,
b	Природы он рисует идеал.
c	Под сенью гор Тавриды отдалённой,
c	Певец Литвы в размер его стеснённый
d	Свои мечты мгновенно заключал.

[1] See p. 58.

> *e* У на́с его́ ещё не зна́ли де́вы,
> *d* Как для него́ уж Де́львиг забыва́л
> *e* Гекза́метра свяще́нные напе́вы.
>
> А. Пушкин

From time to time *terza-rima* (терци́ны) is found too for which Russian poetry is indebted less to the Italians, though it is the verse of Dante's *Divine Comedy*, than to the Parnassians. Although a set form of poetry, terza-rima has no fixed dimensions. It is a sequence of lines in which the first line rhymes with the third, the second with the fourth and sixth, the fifth with the seventh and ninth, and so forth, with the result that each rhyme is repeated three times. Terza-rima is printed in three-line groups and in each the rhyme is enclosing. The metre is usually the five-foot iambic. Except in the translations of the *Divine Comedy*, terza-rima is a rare form in Russian poetry. An example is the opening to the rather mediocre poem *The Song of Hell* (Песнь Ада) by A. Blok:

> *a* День догоре́л на сфе́ре то́й земли́,
> *b* Где я иска́л путе́й и дне́й коро́че.
> *a* Там су́мерки лило́вые легли́.
>
> *b* Меня́ там не́т. Тропо́й подзе́мной но́чи
> *c* Схожу́, скользя́, усту́пом ско́льзких ска́л.
> *b* Знако́мый А́д гляди́т в пусты́е о́чи.
>
> *c* Я на земле́ был бро́шен в я́ркий ба́л,
> *d* И в ди́ком та́нце ма́сок и обли́чий
> *c* Забы́л любо́вь и дру́жбу потеря́л.

None of the set poetic forms in which medieval and Renaissance France abounded, some of which were revived in the nineteenth century, none of the virelays, rondeaux, triolets, and so forth, took root in Russian poetry. Occasionally modern poets have experimented with some of them, rather as exercises in versification, like the following *triolet* (триоле́т) by Fedor Sologub:

A   В не́бо я́сное гляжу́,
B   И душа́ моя́ взволно́вана,
b   Ди́вной та́йной зачаро́вана.
A   В не́бо я́сное гляжу́, —
a   Са́м ли звёзды нахожу́,
b   Бо́жья ль та́йна в них зако́вана?
A   В не́бо я́сное гляжу́,
B   И душа́ моя́ взволно́вана.

This poem is written in four-foot trochaics, but there exist other triolets by the same poet, composed in iambics.

IV

ACCENTUAL VERSE

I. GENERAL REMARKS

ACCENTUAL verse takes into account only the number of stresses per line, which constitutes its one stable element. On the other hand, the number of unstressed syllables, between the stresses, is variable. Therein lies a notable difference from the syllabic-accentual verse. It follows that the concept of the foot has no place in accentual verse.

In theory, the number of unstressed syllables between the stresses is not fixed in an accentual line. In practice, it is more often than not reduced to one, two, or three syllables. Four or five unstressed syllables are rare. Two stresses together are even more rare. The great attraction of accentual poetry therefore is its ability to present, *in one and the same poem*, unstressed intervals of one, two, or three syllables, in a way that syllabic-accentual poetry cannot.

Accentual verse has long been familiar in popular poetry in Russia. This is not surprising: such poetry is meant to be sung and its stresses are in fact musical stresses. However, Russian learned poetry owes little to popular verse and was influenced by it only in the eighteenth century and at the beginning of the nineteenth. But that was the very time when examples of accentual verse were rare in Russian learned poetry.

Regarding any question of influence, that of the accentual verse of the German romantics most readily comes to mind. In German it is a well-known fact that a ceaseless struggle has raged between the syllabic principle, of Latin–

Romance origin, and the purely native principle of accentual verse. Since the end of the eighteenth century German poetry has been invaded by accentual verse. On the other hand, the irregular intervals between stresses also bring Russian accentual verse closer to French verse. It is known, as a matter of fact, that the Russian symbolists, especially those who actually ensured the success of accentual poetry in Russia, were strongly influenced by their French contemporaries.

Yet purely accentual verse can be achieved by a natural development starting from syllabic-accentual verse, in just the same way as the latter grew from a purely syllabic origin.

As it is, a syllabic-accentual line with binary metre can give the impression of an accentual line if the unstressed intervals are long enough and if the number of feet varies from one line to another, in other words if it is a 'free verse' line. Here, for proof, is a trochaic quatrain by Mayakovsky, composed of lines of $8+5+7+5$ feet, giving a somewhat cavalier definition of poetry:

> Нами ли́рика в шты́ки́ неоднокра́тно атако́вана.
> Й́щем ре́чи то́чной и наго́й.
> Но поэ́зия, пресволочне́йшая штуко́вина,
> Существу́ет — и ни в зу́б ного́й.

$$-- | \overset{\prime}{-} - | -- | \overset{\prime}{-} - | -- | \overset{\prime}{-} - | -- | \overset{\prime}{-} - | -$$
$$\overset{\prime}{-} - | \overset{\prime}{-} - | \overset{\prime}{-} - | -- | \overset{\prime}{-}$$
$$-- | \overset{\prime}{-} - | -- | -- | \overset{\prime}{'} - | -- | \overset{\prime}{-} - | -$$
$$-- | \overset{\prime}{-} - | -- | \overset{\prime}{-} - | \overset{\prime}{-}$$

The absence of caesura separates these lines still further from standard trochaic verse. There is a great gulf between this and the melodious quatrain, written in eight-foot trochaic lines, quoted on p. 62:

На́до ве́чно пе́ть и пла́кать ‖ этим стру́нам, зво́нким стру́нам, &c.

But there are other more definite methods of approach, surgical methods one might even say, which obliterate all distinction between the syllabic-accentual and the purely accentual verse.

Indeed, the anacrusis and caesura, with the extra or absent syllables, make a sort of breach in the standard verse. The same applies to the substitution of the iambus for a trochee and of the trochee for an iambus in the first foot of binary verse. The hypermetrical stresses of the initial syllable in iambic, amphibrachic, and anapaestic metres also lead to the same result. Such devices bring out still more the importance of stress and already constitute a step in the direction of accentual verse.

Another step would be to move stress from a strong to a weak syllable, or again, to add or omit a particular syllable *inside* the line, as the author pleases. Poets such as Tyutchev or Fet have achieved this degree of flexibility. Bryusov specialized in the stressing of weak syllables.

There is yet another way of achieving the passage from syllabic-accentual to accentual verse. It consists in combining, in one and the same line, binary and ternary metres. What might be called a kind of Russian logaoed. As such, they might be classified with syllabic-accentual poetry. If, nevertheless, they are grouped with accentual lines, it is because the principle of combined metre is not often observed strictly from one end of a poem to the other. For the slightest deviation from this principle undoubtedly puts these lines in the accentual class. In this connexion it will be observed that imitations of antique metres, attempted occasionally in Russia from the middle of the eighteenth century to the middle of the nineteenth, also lead to accentual verse.

It is evident then that there is no absolutely clear distinction between the syllabic-accentual and the accentual verse.

Accentual verse, in Russia, while making its first appearance in the eighteenth century, became common only towards the middle of the nineteenth century, with poets such as Fet, Polonsky, and others. The symbolists respected it, especially Alexander Blok, the real creator of modern accentual verse. Other poets, such as Akhmatova, Gumilev, Esenin, Mayakovsky, to mention only the most famous, have consolidated and developed the work of Blok. Today, accentual verse is common in Russian poetry, although it was never so widely practised in Russian as it was, for example, in German.

In Russian, accentual verse often bears the name of дóльник, especially in its plural form: дóльники.

II. MODIFICATIONS IN SYLLABIC-ACCENTUAL VERSE

1. *Occasional deviations*

Occasional deviations in syllabic-accentual verse, as has been pointed out, constitute a means whereby this verse may develop into accentual verse. The relevant feature here is not the first foot in the line, which acquires often an extra stress on the initial syllable, but the feet within the line. Only intentional, though sporadic, deviations will be taken into account and not accidental infringements of the metre such as creep into the verse of inexperienced poets. Without doubt, one may see in them a sort of reaction against the rigidity of an implacable metre. Obviously, only great poets can afford to take such liberties without being suspected of crass ignorance. And great poets have taken these liberties, though sparingly. Thus Tyutchev, an undisputed master of syllabic-accentual poetry, achieved much by the use of these effects. Possibly, in his case, these subtleties were imitations of German practice. Here are a few examples:

Молчи, скрывайся и тай $- \acute{} \mid - \acute{} \mid -- \mid - \acute{}$
И чувства и мечты свои: $- \acute{} \mid -- \mid - \acute{} \mid - \acute{}$
Пускай в душевной глубине $- \acute{} \mid - \acute{} \mid -- \mid - \acute{}$
Встают и заходят оне $- \acute{} \mid -- \mid \acute{} - \mid - \acute{}$
Безмолвно как звёзды в ночи — $- \acute{} \mid -- \mid \acute{} - \mid - \acute{}$
Любуйся ими и молчи. $- \acute{} \mid - \acute{} \mid -- \mid - \acute{}$

'Silentium'

The verse is clearly iambic, but, in the fourth and fifth lines on the third foot, the stress is shifted on to a weak syllable, which transforms both into ternary amphibrachic lines. The only feature common to the six lines then is the stress, of which there are three to a line. In the three stanzas composing this poem the same change of metre occurs in the fifth line of the third stanza.

The iambic basis of this poetry is so obvious that Turgenev, while editing the works of Tyutchev in 1854, felt himself obliged to 'correct' the poem in question and to make the iambics regular. This is how he altered the two abnormal lines, the fourth and the fifth, in the stanza quoted:

И всходят и зайдут оне,
Как звёзды ясные в ночи.

It cannot be disputed that these corrections detract considerably from the charm of the poem.

Another poem by Tyutchev shows an example of a different type, in which the iambic basis is constantly undermined by the addition of hypermetrical syllables after the stress:

О, как на склоне наших лет
Нежней мы любим и суеверней . . .
Сияй, сияй, прощальный свет
Любви последней, зари вечерней!

Полнéба обхватѝла тéнь,
Лишь тáм на зáпаде брéзжит сия̀нье;
Помéдли, помéдли, вечéрний дéнь,
Продлѝсь, продлѝсь, очаровáнье!

Пускáй скудéет в жѝлах крóвь,
Но в сéрдце не скудéет нéжность . . .
О ты̀, послéдняя любóвь!
Ты и блажéнство и безнадéжность . . .

„Последняя любовь"

– ́ | – ́ | – ́ | – ́
– ́ | – ́ | + | – – | – ́ | –
– ́ | – ́ | – ́ | – ́
– ́ | – ́ | + | – ́ | – ́ | –

– ́ | – – | – ́ | – ́
– ́ | – ́ | + | – ́ | + | – ́ | –
– ́ | + | – ́ | + | – ́ | – ́
– ́ | – ́ | – – | – ́ | –

– ́ | – ́ | – ́ | – ́
– ́ | – – | – ́ | – ́ | –
– ́ | – ́ | – – | – ́
– – | – ́ | + | – – | – ́ | –

Each stanza begins with a perfectly regular iambic line. The third line too is regular, save in the second stanza, in which it has two hypermetrical syllables. The even lines show a regular iambic beginning, but in the middle they are usually modified by the introduction of hypermetrical syllables. In the diagram these hypermetrical syllables are shown by a plus sign. It seems easier to explain the structure of this poem in terms of an iambic basis, which is the instant impression made by the first line of each stanza, than by regarding its verse-scheme as purely accentual. For in such a case would it be necessary to admit, in accentual verse, rhythmic omissions of stresses, since the number of these varies between three and four per line. Such a theory would not be impossible, but it would considerably and uselessly complicate the conception of accentual verse. It seems that the poet may have wanted to give some twist to the syllabic-accentual metre rather than to build his poem on the scheme of accentual verse. All this helps to indicate how vague is the boundary between the two types of versification.

As a further type, a supplementary, hypermetrical stress on the last syllable of the dactyl, admitting a masculine rhyme without altering the number of syllables, must be pointed out. This phenomenon occurs in the Imperial Russian hymn. Written in two-foot dactylics by Zhukovsky in 1814, and entitled *The Prayer of the Russian People* (Молитва русского народа), it shows, in the first two lines, and in the first two lines only, two final hypermetrical stresses:

Бо́же! Царя́ храни́!	´ _ _ | ´ _ ´
Сла́вному до́лги дни́	´ _ _ | ´ _ ´
Да́й на земли́!	´ _ _ | ´
Го́рдых смири́телю,	´ _ _ | ´ _ _
Сла́бых храни́телю,	´ _ _ | ´ _ _
Всех утеши́телю	´ _ _ | ´ _ _
Всё ниспошли́!	´ _ _ | ´

The other five stanzas of the same poem consist only of regular dactyls. In the stressed endings of the first two lines there is clearly a secondary stress at the dactylic clausula, which is frequent in folk poetry:[1] Zhukovsky had conceived his *Prayer* as a popular song.

2. *Accentual verse resulting from combinations of different metres*

By combining binary and ternary metres a line is produced which still remains quite close to the syllabic-accen-

---

[1] See p. 105.

tual, though it differs in that the intervals between the
stresses contain a variable number of syllables. It is not
hard to understand why this procedure is highly valued by
poets: it enables them, on the one hand, to alternate unstressed intervals of one or two syllables in the same line,
and, on the other hand, to create four-syllable intervals;
neither process is allowed in standard metres. A mixed line
is distinguished from a purely accentual line by the regular
structure of the unstressed intervals. The following example illustrates these points clearly:

> Измучен жизнью, ‖ коварством надежды,
> Когда им в битве ‖ душой уступаю,
> И днём, и ночью, ‖ смежаю я вежды
> И как-то странно ‖ порой прозреваю.
>
> А. Фет

> ‿ _́ _ _́ _ _ ‖ _ _́ _ _ _́ _
> ‿ _́ _ _́   ‖ _ _́ _ _ _́ _
> ‿ _́ _ _́ _ ‖ _ _́ _ _ _́ _
> ‿ _́ _ _́ _ ‖ _ _́ _ _ _́ _

The very regular distribution of stress and the caesura
suggest a ternary basis for this peculiar metre. It may
originate from a four-foot dactylic line with the first stress
shifted on to the second syllable, which gives the combination of an amphibrach and three dactyls, of which the last
is truncated. But it may be regarded also as the combination of one iambic foot and three amphibrachs, or of two
iambic feet and two anapaests. This type of metre, however, can hardly be characterized in traditional terms of
binary and ternary verse. The majority of lines in this
poem are regular in structure, namely 21 out of 24. Two
lines, however, contain twelve syllables instead of eleven,
and one line only ten. But the feature which occurs constantly throughout the poem is the two stresses per hemistich.

Here is another example:

 Révностью жи́знь жива́!   ⌣ – | – ⌣ | – ⌣
Благослове́н уще́рб   – – | – ⌣ | – ⌣
Се́рдцу! Отда́ст трава́   ⌣ – | – ⌣ | – ⌣
Пра́во своё на се́рп?   ⌣ – | – ⌣ | – ⌣   М. Цветаева

The whole of this poem, which amounts to six stanzas, is
built up on this very regular metre, one trochee and two
iambic feet. If one long word, with the fourth syllable
stressed, covers the two first feet, the initial stress is omitted,
as is usual in binary verse. The word благослове́н in the
second line is treated in this way, and also the word поту-
сторо́нних which occurs twice in the poem. In short, this
metre is simply the general application of a familiar device
which has already been examined: the substitution of
trochee for iambus in the first foot.[1]

S. Kirsanov published in 1944 a long poem, Боло́тные
рубежи́, which is throughout its twenty-two stanzas built
up on an original metre, with few irregularities. The
opening lines follow:

Боло́тные рубежи́, || холо́дные рубежи́ . . .
Уже́ не оди́н ноя́брь || тут лю́ди веду́т войну́,
Ужи́ не прошелестя́т || и за́яц не пробежи́т,
Лишь ве́тер нано́сит ря́бь || на За́падную Двину́.

Как ни́зко растёт трава́, || как я́годы ту́т го́рьки!
Вода́ в желоба́х коле́й, || вода́ на следа́х копы́т.
Но лю́ди веду́т войну́, || зары́лись под бугорки́,
У ве́шек ми́нных поле́й, || у про́волочных витко́в.

– ⌣ – | – – | – ⌣ || – ⌣ – | – – | – ⌣
– ⌣ – | – ⌣ | – ⌣ || – ⌣ – | – ⌣ | – ⌣
– ⌣ – | – – | – ⌣ || – ⌣ – | – – | – ⌣
– ⌣ – | – ⌣ | – ⌣ || – ⌣ – | – – | – ⌣

– ⌣ – | – ⌣ | – ⌣ || – ⌣ – | – ⌣ | – ⌣
– ⌣ – | – ⌣ | – ⌣ || – ⌣ – | – ⌣ | – ⌣
– ⌣ – | – ⌣ | – ⌣ || – ⌣ – | – – | – ⌣
– ⌣ – | ⌣ – | – ⌣ || – ⌣ – | – – | – ⌣

[1] See p. 38.

The line is composed of two equal hemistichs, each one showing the combination of an amphibrach and two iambic feet. The first stress of each hemistich is always applied, as it should be with the trisyllabic foot. Similarly the last stress falls regularly, as is usual with a final accent. But within the line the stress on the first iambic foot may be omitted, and frequently is. There follows a sequence of four unstressed syllables which can be achieved only in mixed metres. Once in the entire poem, in the first hemistich of the last line quoted, the first iambic foot is replaced by a trochaic foot (in the word ми́нных).

It must be said at once that these three poems, which show but few examples of abnormal lines, are yet unusually regular for this kind of Russian verse. What is found much more often is quite simply a certain metrical *basis* with more or less important modifications. The poet chooses a metrical design which seems to him to convey the atmosphere of the whole poem, but to which he does not adhere closely. This kind of accentual poetry, whose syllabic-accentual lineage is always perceptible, seems to be more common than purely accentual poetry, at least in the first quarter of the present century.

One of the last poems of S. Esenin gives an excellent illustration of this. Here is the opening:

> Сно́ва верну́лся ǁ я в кра́й роди́мый.
> Кто́ меня по́мнит? ǁ Кто́ позабы́л?
> Гру́стно стою́ я, ǁ как стра́нник гони́мый,
> Ста́рый хозя́ин ǁ свое́й избы́.

> ´‿ ‿ | ´‿ ‿ ‖ ‿ | ´‿ ‿ | ´‿ ‿
> ´‿ ‿ | ´‿ ‿ ‖ ´‿ | ‿ ‿ | ´‿
> ´‿ ‿ | ´‿ ‿ ‖ ‿ | ´‿ ‿ | ‿ ´‿ | ‿
> ´‿ ‿ | ´‿ ‿ ‖ ‿ | ´‿ ‿ | ´‿

The metrical basis of this poem is made up of the combination of two dactyls and two trochaic feet, with a strong caesura in the middle of the second dactyl. The first hemistich is perfectly normal, with its two stresses at regular intervals. The second hemistich is freer, but, like the first, it contains two compulsory stresses. In the second line the stress has shifted and the third line has assumed an extra syllable which makes it purely dactylic in quality. On the other hand, this same poem contains stanzas in which the metrical scheme is fully applied, as for example:

> Та́к мы далёки ‖ и та́к не схо́жи:
> Ты́ молода́я, ‖ а я́ всё про́жил.
> Ю́ношам сча́стье, ‖ а мне́ лишь па́мять
> Снѐжною но́чью ‖ в лиху́ю за́мять.

> ′ — — | ′ — ‖ — | ′ — | ′ —
> ′ — — | ′ — ‖ — | ′ — | ′ —
> ′ — — | ′ — ‖ — | ′ — | ′ —
> ′ — — | ′ — ‖ — | ′ — | ′ —

In Москва́ каба́цкая, another poem by S. Esenin, from which the opening lines are quoted, an anapaestic metrical basis is apparent:

> Да́, тепе́рь решено́! Без возвра́та   ′ — ′ | — — ′ | — — ′ —
> Я поки́нул родны́е поля́.   — — ′ | — — ′ | — — ′
> Уж не бу́дут листво́ю крыла́той   — — ′ | — — ′ | — — ′ —
> Надо мно́ю звене́ть тополя́.   — — ′ | — — ′ | — — ′
> Ни́зкий до́м без меня́ ссуту́лится,   — — ′ | — — ′ | — ′ — —
> Ста́рый пёс мой давно́ издо́х.   — — ′ | — — ′ | — ′
> На моско́вских изо́гнутых у́лицах   — — ′ | — ′ — | — — ′ — —
> Умере́ть, знать, суди́л мне Бо́г.   — — ′ | — — ′ | — ′
> Я люблю́ этот го́род вя́зевый,   — — ′ | — — ′ | — ′ — —
> Пусть обрю́зг он и пу́сть одря́х,   — — ′ | — — ′ | — ′
> Золота́я дремо́тная А́зия   — — ′ | — — ′ | — — ′ — —
> Опочи́ла на купола́х.   — — ′ | — — — | — ′

In each of the first four lines three perfect anapaests occur, and the first anapaest has an emphatic stress on the first syllable, a usual event, as has been demonstrated.[1] In all

---

[1] See p. 52.

the succeeding lines the two first anapaests are absolutely
regular, but in the third there is often a recession of stress,
which gives an iambic cadence to the end of the line. This
ending is sometimes lengthened and sometimes shortened.
In the last line of the extract, a stress on the syllable кý- is
expected. The recession of the stress on the third anapaest
allows ку- to remain unstressed. But if, in the place of
куполáх, there were a four-syllable word, the first syllable
would be stressed, as for example in опочи́ла на кóлоколáх.

The anapaestic opening was frequently employed in the
poetry of Gumilev. One of the favourite metres of this
poet was a line of eight or nine syllables with a stress on the
third and eighth syllables. The four-syllable gap between
these two stresses might receive a stress either on one of the
two intermediate syllables or not at all. The line is therefore composed of an initial anapaest, followed by one anapaest and one iambic foot, or by one iambic foot and one
anapaest, for example:

Я сегóдня опя́ть услы́шал,	$- - \acute{} \mid - - \acute{} - \acute{} -$
Как тяжёлый я́корь ползёт,	$- - \acute{} \mid - \acute{} - - \acute{}$
И я ви́дел, как в мóре вы́шел	$- - \acute{} \mid - - \acute{} - \acute{} -$
Пятипáлубный парохóд.	$- - \acute{} \mid - - - - \acute{}$
Оттогó-то и сóлнце ды́шит,	$- - \acute{} \mid - - \acute{} - \acute{} -$
А земля́ говори́т, поёт.	$- - \acute{} \mid - - \acute{} - \acute{}$

„Снова море"

or again:

Слóвно мóлоты громовы́е	$- - \acute{} \mid - - - - \acute{} -$
Или вóды гнéвных морéй,	$- - \acute{} \mid - \acute{} - - \acute{}$
Золотóе сéрдце Росси́и	$- - \acute{} \mid - \acute{} - - \acute{} -$
Мéрно бьётся в груди́ моéй.	$\acute{} - \acute{} \mid - - \acute{} - \acute{}$
И как слáдко ряди́ть Побéду,	$- - \acute{} \mid - - \acute{} - \acute{} -$
Слóвно дéвушку, в жемчугá,	$- - \acute{} \mid - - - - \acute{}$
Проходя́ по ды́мному слéду	$- - \acute{} \mid - \acute{} - - \acute{} -$
Отступáющего врагá.	$- - \acute{} \mid - - - - \acute{}$

„Наступление"

The anapaestic opening is so marked that the initial syllable of the first anapaest may normally take a secondary stress that is heavy or light. In the second passage such a stress is found in the fourth line of the first stanza. It could also fall on the two словно as well, but in this case it would be noticeably lighter.

Another type of metre used by the same poet has an iambic beginning, followed by an interval of four syllables before the compulsory stress on the seventh syllable. As opposed to the preceding metre, this interval always includes a stress, so that each line always has three stresses. The iambic basis is obvious, for example:

Волчи́ца с па́стью крова́вой	– ´ | – ´ – – ´ –
На бе́лом, бе́лом столбе́,	– ´ | – ´ – – ´
Тебе́, уве́нчанной сла́вой,	– ´ | – ´ – – ´ –
По пра́ву, приве́т тебе́.	– ´ | – – – ´ – ´

„Рим"

Here is another stanza of iambic cadence and regular metrical pattern, composed of alternate lines of four and three stresses:

Не шты́к — так клы́к, так сугро́б, так шква́л,
В Бессме́ртье, что ча́с — то по́езд!
Пришла́ и зна́ла одно́: вокза́л.
Раскла́дываться не сто́ит.

М. Цветаева

– ´ | – ´ – – ´ – ´
– ´ | – – ´ – ´ –
– ´ | – ´ – – ´ – ´
– ´ | – – – – ´ –

The structures of the first and third line are identical, as are those of the second and fourth, in which the second stress is omitted. The fourth line, however, is compensated by incurring a secondary stress, as in раскла́дываться́.

The following lines show a similar iambic basis, but with four stresses per line:

Господь, я знаю, я недостоин, — ´ | — ´ — — — — ´ —
Я сердцем верю, и вера крепка, — ´ | — ´ — — ´ — — ´
Когда-нибудь буду Господний воин, — ´ | — — ´ — — ´ — ´ —
Но так слаба покуда рука. — ´ | — ´ — ´ — — ´

М. Кузмин

In this poem, the metrical basis is slightly less evident than in the previous examples. The first line has only three stresses, but it is possible for the first syllable of the word недостоин to incur a secondary stress. This poem already comes within the category of the purely accentual system, but there is no clear difference between the two.

On pp. 47–48 an example has been given of the Russian imitation of the classical hexameter, each line of which was made up of six dactyls, the last being truncated to make a trochaic ending. This purely dactylic hexameter was typical of the middle of the nineteenth century. It was, however, not the only one which existed in the eighteenth century and the first half of the nineteenth century in Russian poetry. Indeed, in the classical tradition, for every dactyl (– ◡ ◡) in a hexameter a spondee (– –) could be substituted. German imitators of the classical hexameter, notably Gottsched and Klopstock in his *Messias*, realizing this peculiarity, without being able to make use of a spondee in German, replaced it by a trochee. Russian authors naturally adopted this German tradition. This type of hexameter was first used by Trediakovsky in Аргенида (1751), a translation of John Barclay's *Argenis*, and later in the poem Тилемахида, published in 1766, which for a long time discredited the metre. It became fashionable again at the end of the eighteenth century. The proportion of trochees is still very slight in the translation of the *Odyssey* by Zhukovsky: only 123 lines with occasional trochees out of a total of 12,106 lines. The proportion is higher in the translation of the *Iliad* by Gnedich: 2,549 lines with trochees out of a total of 15,690 lines.[1] But the substitution of trochees for dactyls became frequent in the poems which Zhukovsky set out to render in hexameters, not the great classical models, but the prose of *Undine* by La Motte-Fouqué, or the *Knittelverse* (doggerel) of *Nal and Damaianti* by Rückert, or the iambics of *Combat with the Dragon* by Schiller. Here is an example of this informal, not to say colloquial, type of hexameter taken from the Ундина:

> Э́та доли́на, в то вре́мя слы́вшая Чёрной доли́ной,
> О́чень бли́зко была́ от за́мка, а ка́к называ́ют
> Ны́нче её, неизве́стно; тогда́ ж посело́не ей и́мя
> Чёрной да́ли за то́, что глубо́ко средь ди́ких утёсов,
> Е́лями гу́сто заро́сших, лежа́ла она́, что кипу́чий,
> Бы́стрый пото́к, на скали́стом дне́ уще́лья шуме́вший,
> Чёрен меж е́лей бежа́л, и что не́бо нигде́ голубо́е
> В му́тные во́ды его́ не свети́ло . . .

In this passage, though the dactyl is clearly dominant, six trochees are found nevertheless: вре́мя слы́вшая; о́чень бли́зко; была́ от за́мка; Чёрной да́ли; скали́стом дне́ уще́лья.

From the point of view of Russian versification, such dactylic-trochaic hexameters can be classified either as dactylic verse, with occasional variations, or as purely accentual verse: everything depends on the proportion of trochees which they contain. But in no circumstances can these lines be considered as having a mixed metre, because such casual combination lacks a regulating principle.

In his *Epistle on the rules of Russian versification*, 1739, Lomonosov gave an example of a free mixture of iambic

---

[1] The figures are taken from R. Burgi, *A History of the Russian Hexameter*, Hamden, Conn., 1954, p. 132.

feet and anapaests, a perfectly admissible compound in his opinion. The opening lines follow:

> На восхо́де со́лнце ка́к зарди́тся,
> Вылета́ет вспы́льчиво хи́щный Всто́к,
> Глаза́ крова́вы, са́м верти́тся;
> Уда́ра не сно́сит Се́вер в бо́к,
> Госпо́дство дае́т своему́ победи́телю,
> Преси́льному во́д морски́х возбуди́телю.

```
⏑ ⏑ ́ | ⏑ ́ | ⏑ ́ | ⏑ ́ | ⏑
⏑ ⏑ ́ | ⏑ ́ | ⏑ ⏑ ́ | ⏑ ́
⏑ ́ | ⏑ ́ | ⏑ ́ | ⏑ ́ | ⏑
⏑ ́ | ⏑ ⏑ ́ | ⏑ ́ | ⏑ ́
⏑ ́ | ⏑ ⏑ ́ | ⏑ ⏑ ́ | ⏑ ⏑ ́ | ⏑ ⏑
⏑ ́ | ⏑ ⏑ ́ | ⏑ ́ | ⏑ ⏑ ́ | ⏑ ⏑
```

In the diagram, the lines have been split up into feet following the directions of Lomonosov, who regarded them as a combination of iambic and anapaestic feet. But it is evident that today, just as with the dactylic-trochaic hexameters of Zhukovsky, a metre may be regarded as mixed only if the combination is regularly repeated. Every *free* combination of different feet tends to group the metre with purely accentual verse. Lomonosov's poem, therefore, can be regarded only as a composition in accentual verse with four stresses.

In addition, this passage provides an exceedingly rare example of combinations of masculine, feminine, and dactylic rhyming.[1]

III. PURELY ACCENTUAL VERSE

From the transitional types of verse which have just been examined, the next step is to purely accentual verse, that is to say to verse in which it is difficult, if not impossible, to discover a syllabic-accentual basis. But once again there

[1] See p. 134.

is no absolute division between the two types of verse. As the number of unstressed syllables between the stresses is generally one or two, it is always possible to find in certain lines, or parts of lines, elements of syllabic-accentual versification. Even an interval of three syllables suggests a binary metre, with the stress omitted. Perhaps, therefore, the extracts of verse from poems quoted below may be classified by other critics with types previously examined.

Accentual lines normally incur three or four stresses each. There are practically no lines with two stresses: these would unquestionably be identified with syllabic-accentual verse. Lines with more than four stresses would be too long to be determined by the number of stresses alone, without the help of isosyllabism.

1. *Verse with three stresses*

Lines with three stresses are the most usual. Those which occur most frequently have intervals of one or two syllables:

Вхожу́ я в тёмные хра́мы,	_ ´ _ ´ _ _ ´ _
Совершаю бе́дный обря́д.	_ _ ´ _ ´ _ _ ´
Там жду́ я Прекра́сной Да́мы,	_ ´ _ _ ´ _ ´ _
В мерца́ньи кра́сных лампа́д.	_ ´ _ ´ _ _ ´

А. Блок

Intervals of one syllable (seven) predominate over those of two syllables (five).

А чёрное не́бо светла́ло,	_ ´ _ _ ´ _ _ ´ _
Нас окли́кнул кто́-то с моста́,	_ _ ´ _ ´ _ _ ´
Я рука́ми обе́ими сжа́ла	_ _ ´ _ _ ´ _ _ ´ _
На груди́ цепо́чку креста́.	_ _ ´ _ ´ _ _ ´

А. Ахматова, „Побег"

In the above example, on the contrary, intervals of one syllable (three) are much less frequent than those of two syllables (nine). Also the lines are longer than in the previous poem.

Intervals of three syllables are more rare, for example:

Ах, уста́, цело́ванные сто́лькими,	− − ´ − ´ − − − ´ − −
Сто́лькими други́ми уста́ми,	´ − − − ´ − − ´ −
Вы пронза́ете стре́лами го́рькими,	− − ´ − − ´ − − ´ − −
Го́рькими стре́лами, ста́ми.	´ − − ´ − − ´ −

М. Кузмин

This stanza contains intervals in the following proportion: one syllable, one; two syllables, seven; three syllables, two. The lines are even longer.

A less balanced distribution of stress, with occasional intervals of four syllables and two consecutive stresses, is shown in the following passage:

Если во́лк на звезду́ завы́л,	− − ´ − − ´ − ´
Значит не́бо ту́чами изгло́дано,	− − ´ − ´ − − − ´ − −
Рва́ные животы́ кобы́л,	´ − − − − ´ − ´
Чёрные паруса́ во́ронов.	´ − − − − ´ ´ − −

С. Есенин, ,,Кобыльи корабли"

2. *Verse with four stresses*

As with lines of three stresses, the prevailing type contains intervals of one or two syllables:

Де́вушка пе́ла в церко́вном хо́ре	´ − − ´ − − ´ − ´ − −
О все́х уста́лых в чужо́м краю́,	− ´ − ´ − − ´ − ´
О все́х корабля́х, уше́дших в мо́ре,	− ´ − − ´ − ´ − ´ − −
О все́х, забы́вших ра́дость свою́.	− ´ − ´ − ´ − − ´

А. Блок

In this stanza intervals of one syllable, of which there are eleven, greatly exceed those of two syllables, of which there are only four; whereas in the following example intervals of one and two syllables balance. There are eight of each:

Как быва́ло, забу́дешь, что дни́ иду́т,	− − ´ − − ´ − − ´ − ´
Как быва́ло, прости́шь, кто го́рд и зо́л.	− − ´ − − ´ − ´ − ´
И смо́тришь — ту́чи вдали́ встаю́т,	− ´ − ´ − − ´ − ´
И слу́шаешь пе́сни дале́ких сёл . . .	− ´ − − ´ − − ´ − ´

А. Блок

3. *Imitations of three-stress line of folk-poetry*

Accentual verse with three stresses is predominant in folk-poetry and notably in the richest and most abundant type of folk-poetry, the epic song, or the *bylina* (былúна). As the bylina is meant to be sung, the rhythmic structure of its text attains full value and significance only in a musical performance. If, in the present study, the musical aspect of the bylina is not considered, this is because the epic song is relevant here only as the popular prototype of imitations composed in literary poetry. Here is an example of the bylina, taken from the collection published by Hilferding (Онежские былины):

> То Владúмир князь да стóльне-кúевской
> Он скорéнько шёл в столóву свою гóренку,
> Наливáл он чáру зеленá вина,
> Да не мáлу он стопý да полторá ведра,
> Разводúл медáми да стоя́лыма,
> Приносúл-то ён ко Сóловью разбóйнику.
> Соловéй разбóйник Одихмáнтьев сын
> Принял чáрочку от кня́зя он однóй ручкой,
> Выпил чáрочку-ту Сóловей однúм духом,
> Засвистáл как Соловéй тут по солóвьему,
> Закрычáл разбóйник по зверúному,
> Мáковки на тéремах покрúвились,
> А окóленки во тéремах расси́пались
> От негó, от пóсвисту солóвьего,
> А что éсть-то лю́дюшок, так вси мертвы́ лежат;
> А Владúмир князь-то стóльне-кúевской
> Кýньей шýбонькой он укрывáется.
>
> Илья Муромец и Соловей разбойник

Clearly, these are non-rhyming and purely accentual lines. Each line has three stresses, of which the second is the weakest. These stresses are freely distributed, the intervals varying from one to five syllables, with an average of three syllables. The first syllable is seldom stressed. The end of the line is always dactylic and that is one of the most distinctive characteristics of the bylina. In the musical rendering, the last syllable takes a secondary stress, which explains why the dactylic clausula consists often of two words the second of which incurs a weakened or lost stress on the last syllable: зелена вина̋; полтора ведра̋; мертвы̅ лежа̋т. The second word of the clausula may even be a word of trochaic accentuation as normally pronounced, but which changes its stress directly the bylina is sung: одной ручкой; одны́м духом.

Modification of stress is frequent in the bylina, as for example the two stresses Соловей and Со́ловей in the passage quoted. The accentuation in groups of two words, frequent at the clausula, is similarly frequent within the line: Влады́мир князь; скоре́нько шёл; принял ча́рочку, &c.

The passage quoted reveals a definite trochaic cadence with the unstressed intervals of one, two, three, and five syllables. It is the most common type. But other arrangements of stress exist also, in which intervals of two and four syllables are equally possible. An example is shown in this opening of a bylina, taken from the same collection:

> Как во той ли во Йндеи во бога́тыи,
> Как во той ли во Коре́лы во упря́мыи,
> Как во том ли во го́роде Во́лынце,
> Жил-был мо́лодой боя́рской сын да Дюк Степа́нович.

Different cadences may mingle in one and the same bylina, although several bylinas exist in which the trochaic cadence is respected throughout. However, a great deal depends on the preferences and individual technique of the singers. Characteristically, the first imitators of the bylina used quite simply a four-foot trochaic line with a dactylic clausula.[1]

There are also bylinas, or rather historical songs, with a trochaic clausula.

[1] See p. 33.

Literary poetry sometimes imitated the verse of the bylina. A fairly successful imitation as far as rhythm goes, but not as regards vocabulary and atmosphere, is *The Song of the Merchant Kalashnikov* (Песня про царя Ивана Васильевича, молодого опричника и удалого купца Калашникова) by Lermontov, published in 1837, from which a quotation follows:

> Лишь оди́н из ни́х, из опри́чников,
> Удало́й бое́ц, буйный мо́лодец,
> В золото́м ковше́ не мочи́л усов;
> Опусти́л он в зе́млю очи тёмные,
> Опусти́л голо́вушку на широ́ку грудь, —
> А в груди́ его была́ дума кре́пкая.
> Вот нахму́рил ца́рь брови чёрные
> И наве́л на него́ очи зо́ркие,
> Словно я́стреб взгляну́л с высоты́ небес
> На младо́го го́лубя сизокры́лого, —
> Да не по́днял гла́з молодо́й боец.

It emerges thus clearly that Lermontov succeeded in reproducing all the characteristics of the bylina which have been mentioned above, and especially the dactylic clausula spreading over two words, as well as the accentual groups of two words. One of the peculiarities of this poem distinguishing it from the bylina is a pause, amounting almost to a caesura, after the word which bears the second stress. The force of the metre is thereby emphasized.

In the poetry of Pushkin a different non-rhyming line with three stresses and a trochaic clausula is found. The poet used it in twelve of his seventeen *Songs of the Western Slavs*, and in *The Tale of the Fisherman and the Fish*. In Pushkin's mind it was an imitation both of the decasyllable of Serbian oral poetry[1] and of the verse of Russian epic poetry, which includes historical songs of the sixteenth and

---

· [1] Several of the *Songs of the Western Slavs* are adaptations of Serbian epic songs, usually from the *Guzla* by P. Mérimée.

seventeenth centuries, with the trochaic clausula. Unlike
Lermontov's poem, the poems of Pushkin contain no
clausula made up of two words, nor any pause within the
line. On the other hand, the union together of two words
in one accentual group is rare, which explains the relative
frequency of secondary stresses, more easily perceptible
than stresses of the same kind in Lermontov's poem. The
result in these poems by Pushkin is that there is a con-
sciously produced effect of a whole that is less rhythmic
and more 'jerky'. Here is the opening of. *The Tale of the
Fisherman and the Fish*:

> Жил старик со своею старухой
> У самого синего моря;
> Они жили в ветхой землянке
> Ровно тридцать лет и три года.
> Старик ловил неводом рыбу,
> Старуха пряла свою пряжу.
> Раз он в море закинул невод:
> Пришёл невод с одною тиной;
> Он в другой раз закинул невод:
> Пришёл невод с травою морскою;
> В третий раз закинул он невод:
> Пришёл невод с золотою рыбкой,
> С непростою рыбкой, золотою.

What contributes most to the rhythmic cohesion of this
poem is the fixed number of syllables: nine or ten per
line.

The poetry of Pushkin yields yet another poem of a
popular type of which the rhythmic construction is extremely loose: *Parson and his Servant Balda*. Here is an extract
from it:

> Живёт Балда в поповом доме,
> Спит себе на соломе,
> Ест за четверых,
> Работает за семерых;

До светла всё у него пляшет,
Лошадь запряжёт, полосу вспашет,
Печь затопит, всё заготовит, закупит,
Яичко испечёт, да сам и облупит.

The lines differ considerably in length, the number of accents is very irregular, and the whole rhythmic structure of the story consists merely of uninspired rhyming couplets which clearly mark the end of each line. It is probable that, if the poem were written not in rhyming couplets, but with alternate rhymes, the fact that it is a verse composition would pass unnoticed.

It is impossible to disregard in this verse a resemblance to the primitive imparisyllabic verse which had preceded syllabic poetry. It has been stated already that this primitive verse, by assimilating certain folk-lore elements, has survived to the present day.[1] It is from this type of popular poetry, dealing only with frivolous subjects, that Pushkin drew his inspiration in his story. It is unconceivable that he would use the same verse-form to deal with a serious subject.

It is interesting to quote here, in comparison, an example of this popular style, in the ingratiating words of a pedlar:

А вот и я, развесёлый потешник,
Известный столичный раешник,
Со своею потешною панорамою:
Картинки верчу — поворачиваю,
Публику обморачиваю,
Себе пятачки заколачиваю!...
А вот, извольте видеть, город Рим,
Дворец Ватикан,
Всем дворцам великан!..[2]

---

[1] See p. 3.
[2] Русские народные гулянья, по рассказам А. Я. Алексеева-Яковлева, в записи и обработке Евг. Кузнецова. Ленинград-Москва, 1948, p. 55.

4. *Verse with a variable number of stresses*

As in syllabic-accentual poetry, so in the purely accentual poetry, it is possible to imagine equally lines with a regularly alternating number of stresses. For example:

Бе́йте в пло́щади бу́нтов то́пот.	$\acute{} - \acute{} - - \acute{} - \acute{} -$
Вы́ше го́рдых голо́в гряда́!	$\acute{} - \acute{} - - \acute{} - \acute{}$
Мы разли́вом второ́го пото́па	$- - \acute{} - - \acute{} - - \acute{} -$
Перемо́ем миро́в города́.	$- - \acute{} - - \acute{} - - \acute{}$
Дне́й бы́к пе́г.	$\acute{} \, \acute{} \, \acute{}$
Ме́дленна ле́т арба́.	$\acute{} - - - \acute{} - \acute{}$
На́ш бо́г — бе́г,	$\acute{} \, \acute{} \, \acute{}$
Се́рдце — на́ш бараба́н.	$\acute{} - \acute{} - - - \acute{}$

В. Маяко́вский, „Наш марш"

This 'march', ingeniously imitating the beating of a drum, combines two accentual lines of trochaic cadence with two strictly anapaestic lines and ends in a feat of skill with a purely accentual quatrain comprising two trisyllabic lines with three stresses.

Evidently this poem reveals an accentual structure that is variable but none the less very regular. However, in contemporary poetry whole poems exist in which the number of stresses varies from one line to the next. This is, to some extent, the 'free verse' of accentual poetry, comparable with the *vers libre* of modern French poets. An example follows:

В любо́м учрежде́ньи, куда́ ни препожа́луйте,
Слы́шен ладо́ней скри́п.
Э́то при по́мощи рукопожа́тий
Лю́ди разно́сят гри́пп.
Но баци́лла ни одна́ не име́ет пра́ва
Ле́зть на тебя́ без ви́зы Наркомздра́ва.
И над канцеля́рией, в простено́чной те́ми,
Виси́т объявле́ние сле́дующей су́ти:
— Ввиду́ эпиде́мии
Ру́ку друг дру́гу зря́ не су́йте. —

А под плака́том — помглавбу́ха,
Р̆о́бкий, как ря́бчик, и ве́жливей пу́ха.
Прочёл чино́вник слова́ плака́тца,
Реши́л — не жа́ть: на плака́т полага́ться.
Не умира́ть же! И как мышо́нок
Заёрзал, шурша́, в этажа́х бумажо́нок.

В. Маяковский, „Глупая история"

```
_ ´ _ _ ´ _ _ ´ _ _ _ ´ _ _
´ _ _ ´ _ ´
´ _ _ ´ _ _ _ _ _ _ ´ _
´ _ _ ´ _ ´
_ _ ´ _ _ _ ´ _ _ ´ _ ´ _
´ _ _ ´ _ ´ _ _ _ ´ _
_ _ _ _ ´ _ _ _ ´ _ _ _ ´ _
_ ´ _ _ ´ _ _ ´ _ _ _ ´ _
_ ´ _ _ ´ _ _
´ _ _ ´ _ ´ _ ´ _
_ _ _ ´ _ _ _ ´ _
´ _ _ ´ _ _ ´ _ _ ´ _
_ ´ _ ´ _ _ ´ _ ´ _
_ ´ _ ´ _ _ ´ _ _ ´ _
_ _ _ ´ _ _ _ ´ ´ _
_ ´ _ _ ´ _ _ ´ _ _ ´ _
```

Evidently, the number of syllables in a line varies considerably—between six and fourteen. The number of
stresses is normally three or four, but may decrease to two.
The unstressed intervals generally cover two or three syllables, seldom one or four; in the single case of an interval
with five syllables, which occurs in the third line, the
reading must probably be ру́копожа́тий, with two stresses,
so that the line becomes purely dactylic.

One may wonder what remains of a poem, if the lines
are of very different lengths, if the number of stresses is
unstable, and if the unstressed intervals are variable. In
fact, metrically speaking, the verse disappears, that is to
say, there is no metrical principle capable of grouping all
these lines.

In the absence of a metrical structure, the poetic character of such verse is indicated only by rhythmic factors: a not too irregular distribution of stresses line by line with intervals usually balanced, the occasional return of the same rhythm in parallel lines, for example, lines two and four, and lines thirteen and fourteen, a carefully devised arrangement of syntax, and, certainly the most important factor, an unusual and always original rhyme, whereby the end of one line is remembered and linked with the end of the next.

The vital part that syntactical arrangement plays in this poetry is shown by the way in which Mayakovsky had his verse printed, which the passage quoted does not reproduce. The line is broken up into little syntactical or semantic groups, stepped across the page and arranged in rhythmic groups. This kind of poetry, much more than any other, depends for its effect on the manner of recitation. Thus Mayakovsky's attempt to suggest in advance the rhythm with which it should be recited is easily understood. A specimen of such an arrangement follows:

> Гра́ждане,
>> у меня́
>>> огро́мная ра́дость.
> Разулы́бьте
>> сочу́вственные ли́ца,
> Мне́
>> обяза́тельно
>>> подели́ться на́до,
> Стиха́ми
>> хотя́ бы
>>> подели́ться.
>>>> ,,Я счастлив"

Mayakovsky's verse undoubtedly contains the minimum of discipline and organization required by a poem if it is not to degenerate into ordinary prose. Beyond this limit it is hard to imagine verse that may still be regarded as verse and not as rhythmic prose, particularly if it is un-rhymed. This happens, for example, in the *Songs of Alexandria* (Александрийские песни) by Kuzmin:

Когда́ мне говоря́т: ,,Александри́я“,
я ви́жу бе́лые сте́ны до́ма,
небольшо́й са́д с гря́дкою левко́ев,
бле́дное со́лнце осе́ннего ве́чера,
и слы́шу зву́ки далёких фле́йт.

Когда́ мне говоря́т: ,,Александри́я“,
я ви́жу звёзды над стиха́ющим го́родом,
Пья́ных матро́сов в тёмных кварта́лах,
танцовщи́цу, пля́шущую ,,осу́“,
и слы́шу зву́к тамбури́на и кри́ки ссо́ры.

Когда́ мне говоря́т: ,,Александри́я“,
я ви́жу бле́дно-багро́вый зака́т над зелёным мо́рем,
мохна́тые мига́ющие звёзды
и све́тлые се́рые глаза́ под густы́ми бровя́ми,
кото́рые я ви́жу и тогда́,
когда́ не говоря́т мне: ,,Александри́я“.

V

SECONDARY RHYTHMIC ELEMENTS

THE study of the syllabic-accentual verse has entailed a survey of the fundamental elements of the metre, as well as its secondary elements, anacrusis, caesura, grouping of the lines in stanzas, the number of feet in the line, and so forth. Together, these elements make up the metrical scheme of the poem—a scheme which the poet freely accepts. With this scheme as his framework, the poet is still free to some extent to vary its rhythmic patterns and to exploit in particular the possibilities of omitting the stress in binary metres or of adding to the number of stresses in ternary metres.

In the various forms of accentual poetry the metrical scheme exercises a less rigid control which dwindles into insignificance in the peripheral forms.

Whatever scheme is chosen by the poet, the rhythmic patterns, which have been studied hitherto, have been closely connected with the scheme and have proceeded quite naturally from it.

But it would be incorrect to think that the rhythmic elements of the verse are limited to those resulting from the suppleness which every metrical scheme, syllabic-accentual as well as accentual, allows the poet. Lines of verse are composed of words and phrases and these words and phrases exist to be recited. This involves a whole set of considerations regarding phonology, syntax, vocabulary, and semantics, all entirely unconnected with metre, but they are elements which the poet is forced to take into

I

account. A poet worthy of the name not only reckons with them, but even makes use of them to increase the rhythmic effect of his verse. These characteristics of rhythm, quite independent of the metrical scheme, can be called the *secondary elements in the rhythm.*

These elements are less distinct than those relating to metre, and their rendering in certain cases depends less on the poet than on the person who interprets his verse, with the result that they may receive subjective and, sometimes, even contradictory interpretations. Moreover, these secondary elements in the rhythm, which do not proceed from the type of versification itself, are less specifically Russian than the fundamental elements that have been studied up to the present. An examination of them, therefore, will discover in particular characteristics that relate to every type of European versification.

Among these elements, only rhyme shows essentially Russian characteristics. Consequently it will be studied in a special chapter.

I. PHONETIC ELEMENTS

1. *Relative degrees of stress*

So far stress in Russian verse has been regarded from a purely metrical angle, and the study has been restricted to the omission of stresses which the metre would normally demand, or to their irregular appearance in weak syllables. In considering the unwanted appearance of stresses the term 'emphatic stress' has been used.[1] This term has of course absolutely no connexion with any metrical scheme in a line. But in the examples given, the stress on the initial syllable of an iambic, an anapaestic,

---

[1] See p. 38.

or an amphybrachic line, for semantic reasons, succeeds in altering the accentual structure of the line.

Now there may be some semantic stresses, either emphatic or logical, which become apparent only by their degree of accentuation. Thus stresses of varying degrees are created. This inequality of stress, without causing any change in the metrical design of the line, nevertheless influences its rhythmic cadence.

The simplest illustration is that of the ambiguous words, such as various kinds of pronouns and adverbs.[1] The fact that they can appear both as strong and as weak syllables automatically diminishes the value of their stress, even when they occur as strong syllables.

But occasionally the hierarchy of stresses operates in words such as nouns, adjectives, and verbs, whose very nature calls for a full, unambiguous stress. Then semantic considerations alone govern the hierarchy of stress, which is left largely to the taste of the person who interprets the poem. Many poems may illustrate this point, but as an example a quatrain composed of four-foot trochaics is quoted:

> Кто́ меня вражд́ебной вла́стью
> Из ничто́жества воззва́л,
> Ду́шу мне напо́лнил стра́стью,
> Ум сомне́ньем взволнова́л?
>
> А. Пушкин

The first word, кто, may take a heavy stress to make the question more pressing and more personal, but the need for this reinforcement is not very obvious. On the other hand, in the last two lines, it seems that the words стра́стью and сомне́ньем should bear a particularly strong emphatic stress. A possibly less felicitous, but, even so, plausible, variant would be to reinforce the stress on ду́шу and on у́м. It is just permissible to introduce the two reinforcements

[1] See p. 16.

simultaneously, although this might, on aesthetic grounds, be open to question. What is certain is that the two verbs наполнил and взволновал ought to bear distinctly weaker stresses than the nouns surrounding them. Finally, it may be left to the choice of the person reciting to emphasize or not the stresses on враждебной and on ничтожества.

The accentual interpretation of a poem is a matter of personal taste. But it is important to notice that the intensification and, above all, the addition to the number of semantic stresses does not fit in with the actual structure of Russian verse, which is founded on a rather delicate stress pattern.

For this reason the abuse of emphatic and logical stresses may disfigure, if not destroy, the supple metrical pattern of Russian verse, with the effect that the metre is then shattered by semantics. Professional artists are often guilty of that particular violation of taste.

Whatever the relative strength of stresses on the strong syllables, weak syllables must not involve the use of words requiring logical or emphatic stress, which have been forced by the metrical structure of the line into an unstressed position. A reciter, in order to save the metre, has to glide quickly over such words to the detriment of sense. That is the kind of defect which impairs the quality of the verse. Lesser poets incline to this lapse in ternary metres, which readily allow a disyllabic word to be placed between two stresses. Some examples follow:

> Если ж вдруг вспыхнут искры нежданной любви,
> Или на сердце горе накопится . . .
>
> Я. Полонский

> Потянул ветерок — воду морщит, рябит.
> Пронеслись утки с шумом и скрылися.
>
> И. Никитин, „Утро"

Посмотри́: побледне́л серп луны́,
Побледне́ла звезда́ Афроди́ты.

В. Соловьев

In these three anapaestic passages, the words, вспы́хнут, во́ду, у́тки, and серп ought, semantically, to bear the stress, though in fact they occur as weak syllables.

2. *Number of consonants*

In a syllabic-accentual line the number of vowels is fixed as a result of the fixed number of syllables. The number of consonants, on the other hand, is not limited by the metrical design, and, by varying their number, the poet may obtain effects that are purely phonetic and rhythmical. An increase in the number of consonants serves, more often than not, to render the rhythm heavy and slow, a decrease to make the lines more swift and flowing. Poets can wield these contrasts freely, for example, in concluding a quatrain, or other form of stanza, or quite simply a syntactical whole, by a line in which the consonants are reduced to a minimum: such a line will have the same metrical length as all the other lines but, rhythmically, it will be shorter.

An example is contained in the following quatrain of trochaic four-foot lines:

Здра́вствуй, кня́зь ты мой прекра́сный!
Что́ ты ти́х, как де́нь непа́стный?
Опеча́лился чему́?
Говори́т она ему́.

А. Пушкин, „Сказка о царе Салтане"

This procedure is particularly striking when the last line has greater significance from the semantic point of view than the preceding ones, since it brings the syntactical development to its climax, as in the following quatrain of four-foot iambic lines:

> Окóп. Гвардéйцев двáдцать вóсемь.
> Здесь кáждый вспоминáл своé,
> Родны́х, роднóго нéба прóсинь,
> Её, далёкую её.

> Н. Тихонов, ,,Слóво о 28 гвардейцах"

The next example, composed in five-foot trochaics, shows an entirely contrary arrangement:

> Если ты́, такóе óко, смéрклось,
> Знáчит жи́знь не жи́знь есть, смéрть не смéртъ есть.

> М. Цветаева, ,,Новогóднее"

In purely accentual verse, whose number of syllables varies, this device is less effective. It can be supported, in a parallel way, by reducing the number of unstressed syllables.

3. *Alliteration*

Russian poetry sometimes makes use of alliteration (аллитерáция) as a purely phonetic method, for love of what might be described as melodic ornament evoked by the repetition of identical sounds, principally consonants. The great poets of the first half of the nineteenth century scarcely used it at all. With good modern poets, alliteration remains an unusual poetic device employed with restraint. Some examples in four-foot trochaics follow:

> Вóлге дóлго не молчи́тся.
> Ей ворчи́тся как волчи́це.
> Вóлны Вóлги, тóчно вóлки.
> Вéтер бéшеной погóды.
> Вьётся шёлковый лоскýт.
> И у Вóлги, у голóдной,
> Слю́ни гóлода текýт.

> В. Хлебников, ,,Устрýг Разина"

Скро́мный до́м, но рю́мка ро́му
И набро́сков чёрный гро́т,
И взаме́н камо́р — хоро́мы
И на чердаке́ черто́г.

Б. Пастерна́к

In the work of Balmont, whose poetic judgement is often
questionable, alliteration may take quite absurd forms:

Ве́чер. Взмо́рье. Вздо́хи ве́тра.
Велича́вый во́зглас во́лн.
Бу́ря бли́зко. В бе́рег бьётся
Чу́ждый ча́рам чёрный чёлн.

This quatrain is interesting also because it shows foot-
endings coinciding with word-endings.

Alliteration was one of the essential elements of old Germanic poetry, and contemporary German poetry seems
partially to have recovered its former heritage. For alliteration is more common there than in modern Russian poetry,
which cannot fall back upon a similar ancient popular
tradition.

The practice of using alliteration for semantic ends, to
render certain acoustic images or ideas, exists also, of
course. But obviously this kind of lily-painting is confined
to minor poets, who misconstrue the nature and ends of
poetry.

II. SYNTACTICAL ELEMENTS

The essential distinction of verse as contrasted with
prose, is the succession of groups of rhythmic units repeated
in regular order. These groups of rhythmic units are the
lines and, if there is a caesura, the hemistichs. On the other
hand, every poetic work is also composed of syntactical
elements: sentences, clauses, or more limited syntactical
groups.

There are two important connexions between lines of verse and their syntax.

1. *Concordance of syntax and rhythm*

According to Russian tradition, which in this respect scarcely differs from universal poetic tradition, the ends of syntactical groups may not coincide with the ends of rhythmic groups—end of the line and of the hemistich, but, in general, they do not contradict them. In other words, if the syntactical break falls in the middle of a line, it is not normally stronger than the rhythmic break constituted by the end of the line. Here is a typical example in a four-foot iambic metre:

> Пошли, Господь, свою отраду
> Тому, кто в летний жар и зной,
> Как бедный нищий, мимо саду,
> Бредёт по жаркой мостовой.
>
> Кто смотрит вскользь через ограду
> На тень деревьев, злак долин,
> На недоступную прохладу
> Роскошных, светлых луговин.

Ф. Тютчев

The absence of a syntactical break at the end of the first, third, fifth, and seventh lines is not sufficiently distinct to obliterate the rhythmic break. Similarly, the syntactical breaks after тому, in the second line, and деревьев in the sixth line, are too slight to endanger the unity of the line. It will also be noted that in both quatrains the syntactical groups are harmoniously arranged units, each embracing a couple of lines.

More often than not the syntactical structure conforms still more closely to the rhythm by making its own breaks coincide with those of the rhythm: then each line is a syntactical unit. This is what happens most commonly in

Russian verse. An example is given in a stanza composed
of alternate four- and three-foot amphibrachic lines, which
has been taken from a Russian version of Charles Wolfe's
Ode on the Death of Sir John Moore:

> Не би́л бараба́н перед сму́тным полко́м,
>   Когда́ мы вождя́ хорони́ли,
> И тру́п не с ружёйным проща́льным огнём
>   Мы в не́дра земли́ опусти́ли.
> И бе́дная по́честь в ночи́ отдана́:
>   Штыка́ми моги́лу копа́ли . . .
> Нам ту́скло свети́ла в тума́не луна́,
>   И фа́келы ды́мно сверка́ли.
>   И. Козлов, ,,На погребение английского генерала
>   Сира Джона Мура"

A second illustration is contained in the following stanza
in a four-foot iambic measure:

> Когда строку́ дикту́ет чу́вство,
> Оно на сце́ну шлёт раба́,
> И ту́т конча́ется иску́сство,
> И ды́шат по́чва и судьба́.
>   Б. Пастернак

Or, an even better example, in another stanza of similar
structure:

> Дало́ две до́ли Провиде́ние
> На вы́бор му́дрости людско́й:
> Или наде́жду и волне́ние,
> Иль безнаде́жность и поко́й.
>   Е. Боратынский

In *free verse*, the different lengths of the lines derive
precisely from the care taken to make the rhythmic structure of the line conform to its syntactical structure. This
is most clearly evident in the *fable* (басня). An example,
composed in an iambic measure, follows:

> Во́лк, но́чью, ду́мая зале́зть в овча́рню,
>   Попа́л на пса́рню.
> Подня́лся вдру́г весь пса́рный дво́р.

Почу́я се́рого так бли́зко забия́ку,
Псы́ залили́сь в хлева́х и рву́тся во́н на дра́ку.
Псари́ крича́т: „Ахти́, ребя́та, во́р“.
И вми́г воро́та на запо́р.
    В мину́ту пса́рня ста́ла а́дом.
      Бегу́т: ино́й с дубье́м,
      Ино́й с ружье́м.
„Огня́!“ — крича́т. — „Огня́!“ Пришли́ с огне́м.
Мой во́лк сиди́т прижа́вшись в у́гол за́дом.
          И. Крыло́в, „Волк на псарне“

The traditional typographical arrangement of the fable, which Russian has in common with other languages, emphasizes still more strongly the concordance of syntax and rhythm.

Lines showing a parallel grammatical structure are better able to use syntactical means to obtain rhythmic effects. For example, these accentual lines in which four and three stresses alternate:

Сто́лько доро́г пусты́нных исхо́жено
С те́м, кто мне не́ был ми́л.
Сто́лько покло́нов в церква́х поло́жено
За того́, кто меня́ люби́л.
          А. Ахматова

Or in this stanza in five-foot trochaics:

Пу́ля, им отли́тая, просви́щет
Над седо́ю вспе́ненной Двино́й.
Пу́ля, им отли́тая, оты́щет
Гру́дь мою́, она́ придёт за мно́й.
          Н. Гумилев, „Рабочий“

In the latter example, the parallel grammatical structure is rhythmically so strong that it almost eliminates the enjambment between the third and fourth lines. Apart from this, the combining of two contradictory processes—the syntactical parallel and the enjambment—reveals a consummate skill and irresistible charm.

Again the poem by Fet quoted on page 58 in the section on anacrusis shows a syntactical parallel that is perfectly deliberate.

Since the hemistich has the same characteristics as the whole line, the syntactical parallel between hemistichs reinforces both the rhythmic structure and the caesura. This is revealed in the following otherwise mediocre quatrain, composed in six-foot iambic lines:

> Не говори́те мне: ‖ он у́мер — он живёт;
> Пусть же́ртвенник разби́т ‖ — огóнь ещё пыла́ет,
> Пусть ро́за со́рвана ‖ — она́ ещё цветёт,
> Пусть а́рфа слóмана ‖ — аккóрд ещё рыда́ет.
>
> С. Надсон

2. *Opposition of rhythm and syntax: enjambment*

The regular coincidence of breaks in the syntax with rhythmic breaks produces a certain monotony in lines with an unvarying number of feet. A sure way of avoiding this is to transfer the syntactical break from the end to the middle of the line, in short to use the *enjambment*.[1]

A passage taken from Pushkin's *Bronze Horseman*, which is composed in four-foot iambics but not divided into stanzas, will illustrate this point:

> Евге́ний за свои́м добро́м
> Не приходи́л. Он скóро свéту
> Стал чу́жд. Весь дéнь броди́л пешкóм,
> А спал на при́стани; пита́лся
> В окóшко по́данным кускóм;
> Одéжда вéтхая на нём
> Рвала́сь и тлéла. Злы́е дéти
> Броса́ли кáмни вслед ему́;
> Нерéдко кучерски́е плéти
> Его стега́ли, потому́

---

[1] Russian has no native word other than перенóс for this device, and normally makes use of the French term.

Что óн не разбирáл дорóги
Уж никогдá; казáлось — óн
Не примечáл. Он оглушён
Был шýмом внýтренней тревóги.
И тáк он свой несчáстный вéк
Влачúл — ни звéрь, ни человéк,
Ни тó, ни сé — ни жúтель свéта,
Ни прúзрак мёртвый . . . Рáз он спáл
На нéвской прúстани. Дни лéта
Клонúлись к óсени. Дышáл
Ненáстный вéтер. Мрáчный вáл
Плескáл на прúстань, рóпща пéни
И бьáсь о глáдкие ступéни,
Как челобúтчик у дверéй
Ему не внéмлющих судéй.

These lines could be read with particular emphasis on the syntactical pause, thereby causing the structure of the line to disappear altogether: most professional artists do this as a matter of course. But that certainly was not, nor indeed could it be, the intention of the poet who wrote in rhymed lines of identical length and insisted on the proper value of his four-foot iambic. As the line must be respected and kept intact in the face of all other influences, the series of overflowing lines in the passage quoted shows merely a studied effect in prosody of which the object is this apparent break in the rhythm. The artificiality of this device is apparent every time the syntactical pause coincides with the rhythmic pause after the jerks caused by the enjambment.

The break in the rhythm, occurring in a place where no syntactical break is expected, enhances the significance of the word at the enjambment, whether in the part left behind or in the part carried over. The poet might have made use of it for semantic reasons and it is surprising to find that this is not the case. In the passage quoted above none of the words at the enjambment requires special emphasis. Also, words occur in this position which are insig-

nificant from a semantic point of view, like он | не при-
мечáл, or a conjunction cut in two: потомý | что. The
inevitable conclusion is that the enjambment, at least in
the above passage, and in general throughout *The Bronze
Horseman*, is purely a rhythmic trick. There is nevertheless
a reason for this trick. The jerky rhythm, with unexpected
and, in fact, illogical breaks is admirably adapted to the
capricious actions of the madman who is the hero of this
passage.

That does not mean that poets do not use enjambment
for semantic purposes; but it does mean that this method is
less frequent than one might suppose. It occurs, for example, in this four-foot trochaic quatrain:

> Ни полслóва! Дым столбóм . . .
> Ни полслóва! Всé мертвéцки
> Пьют, и, преклонясь челóм,
> Засыпáют молодéцки.
>
> Д. Давыдов, „Песня старого гусара"

Here, пьют, carried over, emphasizes the subject of the
poem, which is the carousal of the hussars.

Another example follows containing semantic enjambment in the last line of a stanza in five-foot trochaic lines:

> В эти дни безвóльно мысль томится,
> А молитва стéлется как дым.
> В эти дни душá больнá одним
> Искушéнием — развоплотиться.
>
> М. Волошин

The force of this enjambment is further enhanced by the
sharp syntactical pause which follows the word carried
over.

Finally, A. K. Tolstoy's hexameters already quoted on
p. 48 also contain an enjambment of a similar kind:

> В кóлокол, мирно дремáвший, ‖ с налéта тяжéлая бóмба
> Грянула. С трéском кругóм от ‖ неé разлетéлись оскóлки.

What has been said about the end of the line, applies
equally to the caesura, where too the absence of a syntactical break may produce effects in the rhythm comparable
to enjambment, as for example:

> Всё тихо там ‖ ещё. Но уж народ
> Спасéние ‖ царéвича провéдал,
> Уж грáмоту ‖ твою вездé читáют.
> Все ждут тебя. ‖ Недáвно двух боя́р
> Борис казни́л ‖ за тó, что за столóм
> Они твоё ‖ здорóвье тáйно пи́ли.

> А. Пушкин, „Борис Годунов"

If it were not known that Pushkin closely observed the
caesura in *Boris Godunov*, it would be tempting to see none
in the lines quoted.

III. THE WORD AND THE RHYTHM

Whatever the metre or the rhythm of a poem, the
thought must necessarily be expressed in words, whence
the question arises—what is the connexion between the
words and the rhythm? Or else, how far do word-divisions
influence the rhythmic pattern of the line? This relation-
ship has varied with the systems of versification known in
Russian.

In the Russian syllabic verse words intervened only
slightly in the rhythmic structure. Only words coming at
the end of the line and at the caesura received a clear stress
and were accordingly emphasized. The remainder of the
line, to safeguard its prosodic nature, had necessarily to
weaken the stresses, so blurring one of the most striking
characteristics of the word and diminishing the effect of
the break between them. The recitation of a syllabic poem,
as has been said already, required a uniform delivery,
marked as little as possible by stress.

Stress recovered its importance in syllabic-accentual poetry. Nevertheless, this did not benefit the autonomy of the word as much as one might have expected. Indeed, the metrical unit of the syllabic-accentual verse is the line, not the word, and the distribution of stresses is generally independent of the pause between words. Thus, even though the natural stress of the word may be fully respected in this poetry, the distribution of stresses at regular intervals rather swamps the word in a continuous rhythmic flow. Also, the syllabic-accentual verse, built upon the repetition of syllabic groups, treats, metrically speaking, all the syllables of a word in the same way. Indeed, whether the syllable is stressed or not, i.e. long or short, it always accounts for half a foot in binary metres and a third in ternary metres, neither more nor less. Such treatment tends to some extent to eliminate differences in quantity, very marked in prose, between the stressed and unstressed syllables, thus infringing the autonomy of the word. A lot also depends on the type of poem in question. Poets who try for harmony in sound effects, for 'melody', such as Fet, Balmont, and, in general, the symbolists with their indifference to the intellectual aspect of poetry, are more inclined to submerge the word in the rhythmic flow. Conversely, the rhetorical type of poem, such as the eighteenth-century ode, or the colloquial type, as for example the poetry of Nekrasov or even, to a certain extent, *Evgeny Onegin*, pays more respect to the autonomy of the word by giving it a certain function in the rhythm.

Thus it cannot be said that the break between words has no influence on the rhythm of a poem. There are some clear-cut examples in which this break is strongly brought out, as when it coincides either with the break between the feet, or with a break in the syntax. Both these alternatives are usually avoided, because both make the line too spasmodic, especially in binary metre. Therefore the poet makes use of them only when he is deliberately seeking an effect of this kind, as in the passage already quoted from Pushkin's *Poltava*:

> Швед, русский — колет, рубит, режет;
> Бой барабанный, клики, скрежет;
> Гром пушек, топот, ржанье, стон,
> И смерть и ад со всех сторон.

Or again in these four-foot trochaic quatrains, which omit one syllable in the second foot of the first and third lines:

> Школьник? Вздор. Бальник? Сдан.
> Ливня, ливня барабан.
> Глобус? Сбит. Ранец? Снят.
> Щебня, щебня водопад.
>
> Всплески! Всплески! Как из шайки!
> Атлас, старься! Грифель, жди!
> В роще — сойки, в роще — зайки,
> В роще — белые дрозды . . .
>
> М. Цветаева, „Крысолов"

To these may be added the quatrains by Balmont on p. 119, by Hippius on p. 67, and by Voloshin on p. 69.

In ternary metres, the coincidence of breaks between the foot and the word, reinforced by a break in the syntax, may produce rhythmic effects which lend themselves to a musical setting. Here, for example, is the opening of a two-foot anapaestic romance, written by Koltsov:

> Обойми, поцалуй,
> Приголубь, приласкай,
> Ещё раз, поскорей,
> Поцалуй горячей.
>
> А. Кольцов, „Последний поцалуй"

This poem has been set to music by nine different composers.

When the limit of a word is not marked by a break in the syntax, the importance of its function in the metrical flow is greatly reduced. In theory, in a four-foot iambic line the different combinations of rhythmic stresses, resulting from the removal of stresses on different syllables, together with the ends of the words, give thirty-eight possible variants. In practice a quarter of them are hardly ever used.[1] Two lines with an identical stress pattern but with a different division into words may produce a slightly different rhythmic effect, as for example in these lines taken from Pushkin's *Bronze Horseman*:

	Адмиралтейская игла́
and	На золоты́е небеса́.

But generally in a line, the breaking up into words is less operative than the distribution of stresses. Hence two lines, with absolutely identical breaks between words, but with the stresses on different feet, will give us a different rhythmic effect:

	О, мо́щный властели́н судьбы́
and	И до́ма то́нущий наро́д.

Conversely, an identical arrangement of stresses tends, to a certain extent, to nullify the difference in the word division:

	И до́ма то́нущий наро́д
and	Пожи́тки бле́дной нищеты́,
	Грозо́й снесе́нные мосты́.

It is, therefore, semantic, and certainly not rhythmic, considerations that make it possible to identify separate words in the flow of a syllabic-accentual line. Apart from semantic reasons, it is not possible to separate the words. Several puns originate from the predominance in the line of the rhythm. In one of these, invented by Gumilev, the

[1] G. Shengeli, op. cit., pp. 139–41.

same five-foot iambic line, therefore the same rhythmic sequence, when recited, may be understood as

Угáр и чáд, в огнé ведрó мадéры,

or as   „Угá", рычáт во гнéве дромадéры.

When this type of line occurs in a poem, it is the neighbouring lines alone which decide its correct interpretation, as in the following lines by Pushkin, taken from the unpublished variants of Chapter VIII in *Evgeny Onegin*:

Порóй лени́в, порóй упря́м,
Порóй лукáв, порóю пря́м.

The sense in which we are to break up the acoustic group *paróyupryám* depends entirely on the meaning conveyed by the first part of the line.

Only this absorption of the individual word into the rhythmic flow of the line justifies the curious telescoping of words which S. Kirsanov uses in his charming *Cinderella* (Зóлушка). For example at the end of this poem:

. . . Потянýлись к Зóлушке чудесá,
Ди́ва ди́вные,
Чýда чýдные,
Чудесá.
Чý, десáнты летя́т парашю́тные,
Чуде-сáльто вертя́т самолёты,
Развернýлась небéс бирюзá!
Чудесáблями брóви,
Чýдесáхаром губы,
Чудесáмые смéлые в ми́ре глазá!

The verse is accentual but, as soon as the poet introduces his trick of telescoping, he breaks into regular anapaests at the word чудесá which provides him with a key and a starting-point. Accentual verse, with its pronounced word autonomy, would scarcely lend itself to such devices.

But this device, as yet employed with reserve by Kirsanov, accounts even so for the first step in the progressive dissolution of the word in the rhythmic flow of the line. The next step would be to invent a rhythmic flow and then to make arbitrary divisions into words. Then all meaning would disappear and nothing would remain but a group of sounds controlled by the rhythmic structure chosen by the poet. This happened after the revolution of 1917 under the pretext of 'liberating' both the verse and the word from its remaining shackles. That is what in Russian is called заумь, or заумный язык, заумная поэзия, of which the English rendering might be 'metalogical' language or poetry, had this term not acquired a precise philosophical meaning.

In its extreme forms such poetry presents nothing but a fantastic group of sounds. In its more moderate forms, it assembles words which do not exist in the language, it is true, but which none the less are conceivable in form, such as nouns, adjectives, and verbs with their inflexions. Thus, all that remains for the poet is to persuade the reader to join him in sharing the delights of this strictly personal idiom, of which the opening lines of the poem Таежная-каторжная by V. Kamensky, in four-foot trochaics, may serve as an example:

> Захурда́чивая в жордубту́
> По зуба́рам сы́пь дурби́нушшом.
> Расхлабы́сть да в мо́рду ту́
> Размордача́й в бу́рд ряби́нушшом.

Words with no sense are here grouped with normal words: together they illustrate the coarse slang of convicts as the title seems to indicate. It must be made clear, though, that this is a moderate illustration of the заумь.

Accentual verse could scarcely adapt itself to such practices. Depending solely on stress, it thereby makes the word emphatic, and the number of its stresses corresponds to the number of autonomous words. In the verse of the Russian symbolists as the examples quoted show, the word does not yet receive its due emphasis. This is not surprising, since the poetry of Balmont, Blok, Akhmatova, Esenin, Kuzmin, and others who represent symbolism as well as the poetic movements which derive from it, are still too much submerged in the rhythmic traditions of syllabic-accentual poetry. The preponderance of the word is revealed more in the work of contemporary poets such as M. Tsvetaeva or V. Mayakovsky. This has already been mentioned at the end of the chapter on accentual verse.[1] Another illustration follows:

> Развева́лся пла́щ его а́лый.
> На щека́х — ю́ность цвела́,
> На уста́х — му́дрость игра́ла.
> Хра́бр как ле́в, стро́ен как тро́сть,
> Ще́др как не́кто, бога́м бли́зкий.
> Ве́чно-пе́рвым наш кри́тский го́сть
> В бе́ге, в бо́е, в мета́нье ди́ска,
> В пе́снях — и в вожделе́ньях де́в . . .
>
> М. Цветаева, ,,Тезей‟

[1] See p. 111.

V I

RHYME

R USSIAN versification, like English and German, employs three kinds of rhyme:

1. *Masculine* rhyme (мужская рифма), with stress on the last syllable, for example, in the following four-foot amphibrachic lines:

> Кругóм как кимвáлы, звучáли скалы,
> И вéтры свистéли и пéли валы.
> Я в хáосе звýков летáл, оглушён;
> Над хáосом звýков носился мой сóн.
> > Ф. Тютчев, „Сон на море"

2. *Feminine* rhyme (жéнская рифма), with stress on the penultimate syllable as in these four-foot trochaic lines:

> Я пришёл к тебé с привéтом —
> Рассказáть, что сóлнце встáло,
> Что онó горячим свéтом
> По листáм затрепетáло . . .
> > А. Фет

3. *Dactylic* rhyme (дактилическая рифма), with stress on the third syllable from the end, as in this four-foot trochaic passage:

> Тёмной тýчей нéбо хмýрится.
> Вся покрыта снéгом ýлица;
> А на ýлице Варвáринской
> Спит . . . мертвéц, мужик комáринский,
> И, идя из хрáма Бóжия,
> Ухмыляются прохóжие.
> > Л. Трефолев, „Песня о комаринском мужике"

Poems giving examples of only one kind of rhyme, such as those from which the above extracts have been quoted, are relatively infrequent. Generally a combination of two sorts of rhyme is found, as occurs both in English and German, and the combination of feminine with masculine rhymes is especially frequent, as is shown in the four-foot iambic lines which follow:

> Несётся конь быстрее лани,
> Храпит и рвётся будто к брани;
> То вдруг осядет на скаку,
> Прислушается к ветерку,
> Широко ноздри раздувая,
> То, разом в землю ударяя
> Шипами звонкими копыт,
> Взмахнув растрёпанною гривой,
> Вперёд без памяти летит.

> М. Лермонтов, ,,Демон"

Other combinations are equally possible, notably that of dactylic rhyme with masculine or feminine rhyme. Here is an example of the latter in a five-foot trochaic measure:

> Сладок холод сердца разлюбившему:
> Он глядит, как в первый день творенья.
> Возвращенье памяти забывшему,
> Ненавидящему — примиренье.

> М. Шагинян

The combination of the three kinds of rhyme in one poem is extremely rare. Lomonosov used it in the poem quoted on p. 101 and Trediakovsky in his Эпиталамическая ода, from which an illustration is given on p. 139. In the nineteenth century a poem by Tyutchev, in four-foot dactylics, serves to illustrate this association:

> Слёзы людские, о, слёзы людские,
> Льётесь вы ранней и поздней порой, —
> Льётесь безвестные, льётесь незримые,

Неистощи́мые, не́исчисли́мые,
Льёте́сь, как льются струи́ дождевы́е
В о́сень глухую́, порою ночно́й.

4. *Hyperdactylic* rhyme (гипердактили́ческая ри́фма),
that is to say rhyme in which the stress comes before the
third syllable from the end of the line, occurs very seldom.
One of the oldest examples, if it is not in fact the oldest, is
found in an amphibrachic poem in lines of two feet by
Delvig:

Весно́ю раско́ванная
Земля́ ожива́ет
И и́м очаро́ванная
Сильне́е пыла́ет
Любо́вью живи́тельною.

„Жаворонок“

The им in the third line refers to the skylark (жа́воронок).
Of the four pairs of hyperdactylic rhymes in this poem, two
only are real rhymes; the other two are merely examples
of assonance. This is characteristic.

Bryusov, who scorns no device in prosody, has in his
repertory some rhymes trailing behind them as many as
five or six unstressed syllables, as, for example, in these
five-foot trochaic lines:

Звёзды, в тёмном не́бе сла́бо вздра́гивающие,
Шта́мбы ро́з, свои цветы́ протя́гивающие.
„Семь цветов радуги“.
Ве́тви, тёмным балдахи́ном све́шивающиеся,
Шу́мы ре́чки, с да́льней пе́сней сме́шивающиеся.
„Ночь“.

But since Russian verse normally does not suffer stress
intervals of more than four syllables, it is clear that such
rhymes cannot dispense with secondary stresses. Moreover,
these rhymes are only exercises in versification, with no
practical significance.

Poems also exist in which only the even lines are rhymed, the odd lines being rhymeless. Unlike English and German poets, the best Russian poets do not normally use this pattern. A specimen follows in four-foot trochaic lines:

> Поле зыблется цветами . . .
> В небе льются света волны . . .
> Вешних жаворонков пенья
> Голубые бездны полны.
>
> А. Майков

Russian poetry abounds in all the rhyme combinations common to European poetry: rhyming couplets (смежная рифма: *a a b b*); alternate rhymes (перекрестная рифма: *a b a b*).; enclosing rhymes (охватная or кольцевая рифма: *a b b a*), to mention a few, and any other arrangement that a poet's fancy might conceive. The examples quoted are sufficient to illustrate the whole variety of these combinations, particularly in the section concerning the stanza.

The mechanism of the standard rhyme is in itself simple in Russian versification. Two varieties need to be distinguished: (1) masculine rhyme ending with a vowel, and (2) all other rhymes, masculine ending with a consonant, feminine, dactylic, and hyperdactylic. The examples which follow have been selected from passages quoted at the beginning of this chapter.

In masculine rhyme ending with a vowel there must be identity between this stressed vowel and the supporting consonant which precedes it:

скалы́	скаку́	змея́ (*zmiyá*)
валы́	ветерку́	моя́ (*mayá*)

In other rhymes, the identity must be between the vowel stressed and all that follows it.

Masculine rhyme:

оглушён	копы́т	свой
сон	лети́т	землёй

Feminine rhyme:

привéтом	оживáет	встáло	лáни
свéтом	пылáет	затрепетáло	брáни

раздувáя	творéнья	вóлны
ударяя	примирéнье	пóлны

Dactylic rhyme:

Варвáринской	Бóжия	разлюбúвшему
комáринский	прохóжие	забы́вшему

Hyperdactylic rhyme:

раскóванная	притя́гиваются	свéшивающиеся
очарóванная	дотрáгиваются	смéшивающиеся

It is not necessary that the sounds which precede the stressed vowel, including the supporting consonant, should be identical except when a masculine rhyme ends in a vowel, but they may help to fill out the rhyme.

The conception of rhyme would have been simple if the notion of what constitutes phonetic identity in the rhyme had not changed considerably in the course of time. The history of Russian rhyme is the history of this evolution in the concept of identity. A rhyme that Lomonosov would have rejected as inferior because it was extravagant might. quite easily have been adopted by Lermontov and yet Mayakovsky might have regarded it as inadequate and rejected it on the grounds of banality. The notions of 'good' and 'bad' in rhyming, as in every other element in versification, are not absolute. They are dependent on the conventions of the age.

II. RHYME IN SYLLABIC POETRY

Syllabic poetry, following the Polish-Ukrainian tradition, used only feminine rhyme. Written at first in Church Slavonic, syllabic verse was recited in the way that Church

Slavonic texts were read, letter by letter, and preserving complete identity between the graphic image of the word and its pronunciation. In these circumstances rhyme was reduced, in the work of Simeon Polotsky, to a graphic identification of the ends of words, starting from the penultimate syllable. Stress did not normally intervene:

> Знаменáти хотя́ще ‖ кóсно стяжáніе
> Богáтствъ бы́ти, скóро же ‖ тѣ́хъ исчезáніе.
> Я́ко зѣлó мéдленно ‖ стяжáнна бывáютъ,
> А многáжды въ еди́нъ чáсъ ‖ въ конéцъ исчезáютъ.
> А́ще же и послýжатъ ‖ до кончи́ны комý,
> Но по смéрти нуждá есть ‖ лиши́ти инóму.
>
> „Богатство"

It will be seen that in this passage the words комý and инóму are rhymed in spite of their different stresses; likewise the words стяжáніе and исчезáніе, following convention entirely, constitute a feminine rhyme, and not a dactylic rhyme, a variety which is not recognized in this poetry.

In Ukrainian syllabic poetry the only concessions to living pronunciation were the phonetic identity of ѣ and i, as well as of и and ы. Russian syllabic poetry abandoned the identity of ѣ and i, but kept that of и and ы. In the poetry of Simeon Polotsky for instance:

> Престáните, и́ноцы, ‖ сія́ злá твори́ти,
> Тщи́теся дрéвнимъ отцéмъ ‖ святы́мъ тóчни бы́ти.
>
> „Монахъ"

> Узри́ши ещé въ ри́зы ‖ крáсны облечéнны,
> Иже во убóжество ‖ пóлное стрижéни.
>
> Ibid.

During the eighteenth century, in the syllabic poetry of Kantemir and Trediakovsky, rhyme continued to be exclusively feminine, if this is understood according to the modern interpretation of the word. For it now involves the use only of words whose stress really falls on the penultimate syllable. The identity of и and ы remained intact, on condition, however, that the two sounds did not occur at the absolute end of the line which would create, among the preceding consonants, a divergence between soft and hard:

> Уме, недозрелый плод ‖ недолгой науки!
> Покойся, не понуждай ‖ к перу мои руки:
> Не писав летящи дни ‖ века проводити
> Можно, и славу достать, ‖ хоть творцем не слыти.
>   А. Кантемир, „К уму своему"[1]

III. STANDARD RHYME

The change from the syllabic to the syllabic-accentual system was marked by the introduction of masculine rhyme, alongside feminine rhyme which had been inherited from the previous age. It was found as far back as the early works of Lomonosov who, it would seem, even imported the principle of alternating masculine and feminine rhyme from German poetry.

Dactylic rhyme appeared at the same time, but very hesitantly, becoming perceptible in the lengthening of the feminine rhyme in trochaic verse. For example, it is found in Trediakovsky's Эпиталамическая ода, published in 1751, a translation, which is virtually an adaptation, of a Latin epithalamium in John Barclay's *Argenis*, a pair of dactylic rhymes in every one of the thirteen four-foot stanzas comprising the ode. The fifth stanza follows:

> Зри, жених, всем одаренный,
> В предизбранной красоте
> Зрак Минервин озаренный,
> Взор Юнонин в высоте.

---

[1] For other examples of rhyme in syllabic poetry, see pp. 4–6, 10, 143.

Цитере́ины прия́тности,
Что превы́ше верoя́тности;
Зри, невéста коль твоя́
И Диáну превосхóдит,
Из дубрáв в Ефи́р как всхóдит
Дéвства с чéстию сия́.

Dactylic rhyme was not used systematically until later, when ternary metres were recognized in Russian versification.

Throughout the eighteenth century rhyme still bears the traces of the syllabic, Church Slavonic, tradition of verse-reading, which took account only of the orthographical value of letters, with the one exception that has been noted, the identity in rhyme of и and ы. As a result of this Church Slavonic tradition, the modifications in vowel pronunciation caused by the stress are certainly not used in Russian poetry at any time in the eighteenth century.

Thus the eighteenth-century poets do not rhyme, as a rule, a and o, e and и unstressed and they reject, at any rate at first, the pronunciation of e as ё. So there are no rhymes like сáда : нáдо, кóлет : мóлит, вопрóс : принёс; on the other hand, there are examples of небéс : принéс. But it must be admitted that the rhyme o : ё had already begun to appear in Russian poetry in the eighteenth century and that towards the end of the century it was fairly common. The extent to which it appeared varied according to the different types of words employed.

Dislike of the rhymes a : o and e : и unstressed was more deeply rooted, so much so that early-nineteenth-century poets are still ignorant of them, especially the first pair: Boratynsky and Delvig have no examples of the rhyme a : o, Yazykov has two only, and even Pushkin employs it on only twenty-one occasions. The first poets to put it to regular use are Lermontov and Tyutchev.[1] That means simply that the style of verse-reading changed in the 1830's; it ceased to be Church Slavonic and became purely Russian, conforming to Moscow pronunciation, and thereby losing its artificial character. Such a development shows how dangerous it is to draw conclusions about the real pronunciation of Russian from the state of rhyme in the eighteenth and early nineteenth centuries. Evidently, Boratynsky, who, in his poetry, never rhymed an unstressed a and o, mingled them when speaking his mother-tongue. Rhyme may coincide with the real pronunciation, but usually it only shows us how to read the lines. Which may be a more or less artificial procedure.

Thus it was in the 1830's that the foundations were laid of Russian standard rhyme, as it appears in the examples quoted at the beginning of this chapter. Based on the actual Moscow pronunciation, this rhyme involves the identity of a and o, and of e, и, and я unstressed, as well as the existence of ё as the equivalent of o in rhyme.

To some extent, it likewise recognizes the identity of a, o, and ы after the stress in a close syllable, almost exclusively in case-endings, as росúстым : свúстом in the poetry of Lermontov.

Regarding consonants, standard rhyme requires their complete phonetic, but of course not orthographical, identity: глушь : муж, восхóд : идёт, злúтся : лúца, &c. It follows that a hard and a soft consonant cannot rhyme, and rhymes like конь : стон, чáры : твáри are, if not excluded, at least very much the exception.

Nor does the standard tradition allow the rhyme to be truncated, that is to say a word ending in a consonant to be rhymed with one ending in a vowel, such as взóром : скóро,

---

[1] V. M. Zhirmunsky, Рифма, ее история и теория, Петроград, 1923, p. 157.

a device that has become so common in contemporary poetry. Words in -й are the one exception to this rule, but only when the rhyme is feminine. Examples of this are common from the eighteenth century onwards: Минéрвы:пéрвый in the poetry of Derzhavin, высóкий:порóки, удáры:я́рый in that of Lermontov. Here, representing the first half of the nineteenth century, are some specimens of rhyme taken from Lermontov's *Borodino*: лю́ди:орýдий, готóвы:нóвый, летýчий:тýчи, including some in which the nominative singular of the masculine adjectives should be pronounced *aj* and not *yj*: избúтый:сердúто, немáло:удáлый. This is not allowed in masculine rhyme, that is to say rhyme in which the final -й is in a strong position, after the stress. No poet of this period will, for example, rhyme окнó with знóй.

Poets in the middle of the nineteenth century, without modifying the consonants in the rhyming system, still managed to give more flexibility to the rhyming of the vowels. In the work of a poet such as A. K. Tolstoy, the phonetic identity of vowels is strictly observed only at the stress. It no longer counts outside the stress, in rhymes like:

нáша	двóе	сегóдня
крáше	бородóю	пригóдней

сурóвым	аксамúта	держáвы
слóвом	обвúты	лукáво

лю́бо	гóрдо
дýбу	мóрду

Rhymes of this type are far from being in a majority, but they are now accepted.

During this period, too, poets, by spreading the rhyme over two words, use the broken rhyme effect for punning. For example, in this passage of four and three-foot amphibrachic lines:

Садко́, мое ча́до, уж о́чень ты гру́б,
Не нра́вится ре́чь мне така́я;
Когда́ бы твою́ не цени́л я игру́ б,
Ного́й тебе да́л бы пинка́ я.

                    А. К. Толсто́й, „Садко“

Other rhymes of this type from the work of the same poet follow:

| хвала́ вам | возьму́сь ли | суро́вый | что́ ж | серди́то |
| велича́вым | гу́сли | почто́ вы | проживёшь | Ильи́ то |

In the same way is achieved the studied effect of the following rhyme by L. Mey, composed in three-foot iambic metre, with a trochee at the opening of the first line:

Во́т-с, господи́н Аско́ченский,
Изво́льте-с: вам на́точен-с кий!

The earliest examples of broken rhyme occur only in humorous poetry, that is to say where the poet is deliberately joking.

Occasionally such rhymes for punning are encountered as early as the seventeenth century, and even in the work of Simeon Polotsky:

Е́ллиномъ бога́тствъ бо́гъ бѣ, ‖ наречённый Плу́тонъ;
А́зъ его именую : ‖ во и́стину плу́тъ онъ.

                    „Богатство“

IV. MODERN RHYME

Poets of the present century, especially those writing after 1920, were the first to alter the system of rhyming consonants, which had not been modified since the eighteenth century. It has been shown that the identity of consonants was strictly observed in the rhyme with the single exception of omitting the final *yod* (й) in a feminine rhyme. This exception has been extended by contemporary poets to cover other final consonants, and in due course, a truncated rhyme has come to be recognized. And though it is true that this occurred, sporadically, in the work of Derzhavin (Потёмкин : потóмки), a poet whose technique is surprisingly in advance of his time, as well as in the writings of a few early nineteenth century poets, such as Gnedich (унылым : могилы), these were merely examples of unusual flights of fancy[1].

During the present century the feminine truncated rhyme has come to be practised widely by the majority of poets. Some examples follow, selected from the works of different poets:

A. Akhmatova

мéлких	встрéчей	тревóжит	спрячу
стрéлки	вéчер	Бóжий	плáчет
ýмер	учтивость	встрéтить	
дýме	полуленúво	свéте	

S. Esenin

продýмал	чáщи	бýдет	колóсья
угрюмый	уходящих	люди	óсень
схóжи	причáстьем	заплáкал	нéбо
прóжил	счáстья	собáкой	нé был

V. Mayakovsky

лéса	нáсыпь	смотрéл как
слéсарь	ананáсы	тарéлка

M. Tsvetaeva

перебóев	товáром	рёбра
любóю	Каррáры	дóбрым

A. Tvardovsky

трáтить	прáздник	канáва	навáром
кровáти	рáзный	задáвит	с жáру

[1] В. Tomashevsky, „К истории русской рифмы", Труды Отдела новой русской литературы, 1 (1948), p. 250.

But if a consonant, in feminine rhyme, no longer has any importance, not only a truncated rhyme may be expected, but one with different final consonants. It is understood that the consonants in question must not belong to categories too different from one another. Here are a few examples:

S. Esenin

же́нщин	о́сени	си́лы	му́часъ
ме́ньших	бро́сили	краси́вый	у́частъ

M. Tsvetaeva

просто́ю	со́бран	коло́сьях	чужезе́мцам
престо́ла	до́брым	но́сят	Вифлее́мской
спроси́ла	по́ три	ра́вных	пра́вом
Росси́я	о́тлил	пра́внук	кра́бом

A. Tvardovsky

поглу́бже	фе́рмы	уда́рить	то́чка	похо́да
голу́бчик	наве́рно	па́рень	то́чно	пехо́та

It will be observed that truncated rhyme and the rhyming of different final consonants apply less commonly in masculine rhyme:

S. Esenin   Akhmatova

позабы́л		тебе́
избы́		голубе́л

M. Tsvetaeva

осты́в	сонм	горд
шесты́х	сон	горб

A. Tvardovsky

во вторы́х	бойцо́в	заста́л	просты́л
стари́к	лицо́м	на поста́х	просты́м

S. Kirsanov

песо́к	да ру́к	вида́л	ведра́	в волоса́х
усо́в	дыру́	вода́	видна́	полоса́

Mayakovsky has made considerable use of this development:

глаза́	уста́л	темнота́	нег	по́л
каза́рм	моста́	так	негр	депо́

In dactylic rhymes, the relations between consonants can be made even freer:

M. Tsvetaeva

хлопо́чется	съедо́бное	здоро́вится	вы́сечен
по́шлости	подо́бием	со́вести	стоты́сячной
сча́стливы	о́строве		
тя́жче ли	сёстрами		

S. Kirsanov

щёлочи	кра́бики	во́здуха	ла́ковые
Зо́лушки	кра́пинки	о́тдыха	ра́ковины (hyperdactylic rhyme)

M. Kuzmin

а́исты
ака́фисты

According to general standards these are rhymes no longer, but simply assonances; so that it is true to say that assonance is now on the same footing as rhyme and fulfils the same purposes. However, bearing in mind the internal evolution of Russian verse, it seems preferable to retain the term rhyme to cover such examples of assonance.

Every kind of rhyme considered up to the present, whatever the differences of consonants and vowels, has been invariably isosyllabic. The next step is to rhyme lines in which the final stress does not fall on the same syllable, beginning from the end of the word. The majority of poets, it must be said, refuse to take such a step. However, it has not deterred Mayakovsky, in whose work there are plenty of specimens of heterosyllabic rhyming. In practice, there are two rhyme combinations: dactylic+feminine and hyperdactylic+dactylic. Mayakovsky generally creates such combinations by ignoring the vowel immediately after the stress, for example:

го́роде	ло́паться	обе́д она	э́таких
мо́рде	хло́пца	ме́дных	жаке́тке
то́мики	на́голо	о́хала	доно́сится
пото́мки	на́гло	загло́хла	победоно́сца
обнару́живая	подве́шенного	го́ры нести	
ору́жие	про ве́шнего	поко́рности	

A certain logic in this rhyming cannot be denied, when it is realized that the syllable after the stress, namely the one which Mayakovsky drops, is one of the weakest syllables in a Russian word.

Far less frequently Mayakovsky disregards the final syllable of the word:

| в алфа́вите | нэпа́чка | изна́шиваешь | попа́хивая |
| лафа́ ведь | не па́чкая | на́шего | папа́хи |

Had all these varieties—truncated, heteroconsonantal, and heterosyllabic rhyming—simply been grafted on to standard rhyme, they would no doubt have prevented it from working properly. Yet every example of rhyming given here, taken from the works of the best contemporary poets, conveys not the slightest impression of poverty, but, on the contrary, an effect of richness and resonance. How do these poets succeed in producing such an effect? The answer is fairly simple. In standard rhyme only the sounds following the stressed vowel counted, and, in the case of a masculine vowel rhyme, the previous or supporting consonant as well. In the new rhyme, on the contrary, poets try hard to achieve the richest possible identity of consonants before the stressed vowel. This identity partly makes up for the ravages caused by the technique in the unstressed part of the rhyme. The weight of the rhyme may be described henceforth as being distributed on both sides of the stressed vowel. On referring to the examples quoted it will be agreed that in the majority of them the consonants preceding the stress, and sometimes entire syllables, are identical. Such a development reinvigorates rhyme and lifts it out of the necessarily limited and increasingly depreciating repertory of standard rhyme.

A deliberate quest for rhyme is a general characteristic of contemporary poetry, in which again Mayakovsky is the supreme virtuoso. Not content with employing the technique described, he seeks other ways of imparting originality, and, indeed, extravagance, in rhyming. One of his methods is to rhyme words that are normally unstressed, such as prepositions and conjunctions, for example:

> Угрюмый дождь скосил глаза.
> А за
> решёткой
> чёткой
> желéзной мысли проводóв
> перина.
> Й на
> неё встающих звёзд
> легкó упёрлись нóги.   „Утро"

Another way of enhancing the value of the rhyme is to use the broken rhyme, of which the common practice, and possibly the origin, go back to the middle of the nineteenth century. Modern poets are quite ready to use it, and in the beginning continue to introduce it with a touch of humour, as in the following anonymous couplet:

> Мнé бы было интерéсней
> Повидáться в сентябрé с ней.

N. Gumilev is famous for having invented, with no

serious motive, however, a rhyme pun that is spread across
eight syllables in five-foot trochaics:

> Слы́ша с|ви́ст и во́й локомоби́ля
> Две́рь линг|ви́сты во́йлоком оби́ли.

But one feature of contemporary poetry is precisely the
introduction of this device, whose original purpose was
humorous, into the current repertory of versification. The
following four-foot trochaic quatrain by Bryusov, in content anything but humorous, gives some evidence of this:

> Рве́тся ве́тер одича́лый,
> Бу́ря зна́к дае́т пого́нь . . .
> С бу́рей спо́ря — ро́дич а́лый —
> Ма́шет со́тней ла́п ого́нь.

Mayakovsky, again, applied this device with consummate skill. Such rhymes are innumerable in his poetry.
Here are examples:

га́лстук	ввы́сь поведи	А́фрику	де́шево
услыха́л стук	в и́споведи	ста́в в реку	найде́шь его
шаги́ коня	притти́ вам	за́ сто	
ги́канье	губкооперати́вам	носа́стых	

Obviously, this sort of rhyme attracts our attention by
its originality. In broken rhyme, the second word,
almost without exception, takes a final stress. The final
stress calls for a secondary final stress on the second, non-
compound, part of the rhyme, which gives it particular
emphasis. To obtain this effect there must of course be a
broken rhyme in the first place. Looked at from this
point of view, the following quatrain in three-foot iambics
by Mayakovsky is a masterpiece of ingenuity:

> Глаза́ми взви́ла ввы́сь стрелу́.
> Улы́бку убери́ твою.
> А се́рдце рве́тся к вы́стрелу.
> А го́рло бре́дит бри́твою.

While broken rhyme is rather in favour, the rhyming of homonyms in Russian poetry has never been anything but an exercise in versification, designed to appeal to the public taste for virtuosity. Here is an example in a four-foot iambic measure:

> Ты бе́лых лебеде́й корми́ла,
> Отки́нув тя́жесть чёрных ко́с.
> Я ря́дом плы́л, сошли́сь корми́ла,
> Зака́тный лу́ч был стра́нно ко́с.
>
> В. Брюсов

The following passage illustrates the conception of rhyme held by modern poets, a conception, however, which stops short of Mayakovsky's heterosyllabic rhyming. It is taken from the poem Новогоднее by Marina Tsvetaeva, published in 1927 and dedicated to the memory of Rainer Maria Rilke who had died on 29 December 1926. This poem is written in five-foot trochaics, with some displacement of stress:

> Перебра́сываюсь. Ча́стность. Сро́чность.
> Но́вый Го́д в дверя́х. За что́, с кем чо́кнусь
> Через сто́л? Чём? Вместо пе́ны — ва́ты
> Кло́к. Заче́м? ну, бьёт — а при чём я́ тут?
> Что́ мне де́лать в нового́днем шу́ме
> С э́той вну́треннею ри́фмой: Ра́йнер — у́мер.
> Если ты́, тако́е о́ко сме́рклось,
> Зна́чит, жи́знь не жи́знь есть, сме́рть не сме́рть есть.
> Зна́чит — тми́тся, допойму́ при встре́че! —
> Не́т ни жи́зни, не́т ни сме́рти, — тре́тье,
> Но́вое. И за него́ (соло́мой
> Застели́в седьмо́й — два́дцать шесто́му
> Отходя́щему — како́е сча́стье
> Тобо́й ко́нчиться, тобо́й нача́ться!)
> Через сто́л, необозри́мый о́ком,
> Бу́ду чо́каться с тобо́ю ти́хим чо́ком
> Сткла́ о сткло́? Не́т — не каба́цким и́хним:
> Я́ о ты́, слия́сь даю́щих ри́фму:
> Тре́тье.

As rhyme has developed in Russian, stressed vowels have strictly maintained their identity, whereas the relationships of consonants have become noticeably more simple and closer to assonance. In theory one might expect also a contrary development: the complete identity of consonants together with a difference between stressed vowels. This has not occurred. However, some poets have been tempted by it and have composed some 'rhymed' poetry that follows this principle. Two specimens are given here as a matter of interest.

The opening of a poem by Z. Hippius, with the significant title Негласные рифмы, composed in accentual lines with four stresses:

> Хо́чешь зна́ть, почему́ я ве́сел?
> Я́ опя́ть среди ми́лых чи́сел.
> Ка́к споко́йно меж ци́фр и ме́р.
> Стро́г и стро́ен их ве́чный ми́р.

An entire poem by Igor Severyanin in which the poet has practised great technical skill and exhausted all the vowel resources of one combination:

> Заберу́сь на рассве́те ‖ на сере́бряный ке́др
> Любова́ться отту́да ‖ на мане́вры эска́др.
> Со́лнце, у́тро и мо́ре! ‖ Как я ве́село бо́др,
> Точно во́здух — безду́мен, ‖ точно му́мия — му́др.
> Кто просла́влен орла́ми, ‖ — ах, тому́ не до вы́др!

This poem, written in four-foot anapaestic lines, with an initial hypermetrical stress on the third line, contains also a supplementary syllable before the caesura, following the pattern:

$$- - \acute{} \,|\, - - \acute{} \,|\, + \,\|\, - - \acute{} \,|\, - - \acute{}$$

V. UNRHYMED VERSE

According to the Russian poetic tradition the unrhymed verse line (бéлый стих) is confined to three
types of poetry.

1. It is found first of all in plays written in five-foot
iambics, i.e. in the Shakespearian blank verse line first employed by Zhukovsky in his translation of Schiller's *Maid
of Orleans* and made famous by Pushkin in *Boris Godunov*.
The absence of rhyme in this verse is explained by the fact
that it is a faithful imitation of German and English prototypes.[1]

2. Unrhymed verse is compulsory in the imitations of
ancient metres, notably of the hexameter and elegiac
couplet, which prevailed in the second half of the eighteenth
century and at the beginning of the nineteenth. These,
however, were never really popular.[2]

3. Finally, unrhymed verse is usual in imitations of
folk-poetry, whether of the bylina, such as *The Song of the
Merchant Kalashnikov* by Lermontov, and *The Tale of the
Fisherman and the Fish* by Pushkin, or of popular songs, such
as those imitated by Koltsov.[3]

It is clear that the absence of rhyme is explained by
adoptions made from types of prosody other than those of
Russian learned poetry, whether from foreign sources, German, English, or Greek, or from Russian folk-poetry. This
is proof that unrhymed verse is regarded as something
foreign to the tradition of learned poetry in Russia. Accordingly, its use is rare, except in the types of poetry mentioned, and the poems by Pushkin and Lermontov, for
example, in which it occurs, are few in number.

[1] Examples are found on pp. 22–24, 61, 126.
[2] Examples are given on pp. 48, 66, 100.
[3] Examples of these are given on pp. 33–35, 106–108.

One Russian poet only employed unrhymed verse regularly, namely Zhukovsky. Apart from the long poems that he usually composed in hexameters or five-foot unrhymed iambics, he has left a great many short poems in unrhymed verse. Here, for example, is the opening of his version of the *Stabat Mater*, which is composed in unrhymed four-foot trochaics despite the tail-rhymed stanzas of the Latin original by Jacopone da Todi, which is given here together with the Russian version:

Го́рько пла́ча и рыда́я,	Stabat mater dolorosa
Предстоя́ла в сокруше́нье	Juxta crucem lacrimosa,
Ма́терь сы́ну на кресте́;	Dum pendebat filius.
Ду́шу, по́лную любо́ви,	Cuius animam gementem,
Сожале́нья, сострада́нья,	Contristantem et dolentem,
Растерза́л ей о́стрый ме́ч.	Pertransivit gladius.

However, Nekrasov, an indefatigable experimenter in rhyme combinations, has left us one long poem, which is far from being a masterpiece, written in unrhymed verse: *Who is happy in Russia* (Кому на Руси жить хорошо). Composed in three-foot iambics, the lines contain a dactylic clausula, introducing a stressed ending at intervals of every three or four, and very occasionally two, lines. This clausula, as has been indicated, is typical in popular poetry; also the subject and its treatment come fairly close to folk tradition. These reasons are sufficient to explain why Nekrasov abandoned rhyme in this poem. Here is an extract from it:

Свали́в беду́ на ле́шего,
Под ле́сом, при доро́женьке
Усе́лись мужики́.
Зажгли́ костёр, сложи́лися,
За во́дкой дво́е сбе́гали,
А про́чие поку́дова
Стака́нчик изгото́вили
Берёсты понадра́в.

Приспѣ́ла ско́ро во́дочка,
Приспѣ́ла и заку́сочка —
Пиру́ют мужички́!
Косу́шки по́ три вы́пили,
Поѣ́ли — и заспо́рили
Опя́ть: кому́ жить ве́село,
Вольго́тно на Руси́?

In contemporary poetry the use of unrhymed verse is infrequent. Each time it occurs it gives an impression, not of simplicity, but of a device chosen deliberately to impress the reader. Here are two examples. One is composed in a five-foot iambic metre of which the structure is completely traditional:

И на мосту́, сквозь ржа́вые пери́ла
Просо́вывая ру́ки в рукави́чках,
Корми́ли де́ти пе́стрых жа́дных у́ток,
Что кувырка́лись в про́руби черни́льной.

А. Ахматова

The other example is composed in an accentual measure with three stresses:

Моё окно́ выходи́ло в са́д,
И в су́мерки, сквозь листву́,
Синѣ́ли га́зовые рожки́
Над вы́весками пивны́х.

Э. Багрицкий, „Послѣдняя ночь“

The part played by rhyme is greater in accentual verse than in verse of the standard type,[1] and the absence of rhyme can even have the effect of turning it into rhythmic prose. If, in the example chosen, the reader nevertheless has the impression of well ordered verse, that is because the number of syllables is fixed $(9+7+9+7)$ and the stresses are not of too unusual a pattern; indeed, the even lines incur identical stresses.

[1] See p. 111.

More freedom in the distribution and number of stresses, as well as in the number of syllables, transforms unrhymed verse into rhythmic prose. Among modern poets, Blok, Akhmatova, and Kuzmin employ it a good deal. An extract from Kuzmin's rhythmic prose has already been quoted.[1] A similar passage from Blok follows:

> Впро́чем, она захоте́ла,
> Чтобы я чита́л ей вслу́х Макбе́та.
> Едва́ дойдя́ до „пузыре́й земли́",
> О кото́рых я не могу́ говори́ть без волне́ния,
> Я заме́тил, что она то́же волну́ется
> И внима́тельно смо́трит в окно́.
> Оказа́лось, что большо́й пёстрый ко́т
> С трудо́м ле́пится по кра́ю кры́ши,
> Подстерега́я целу́ющихся голубе́й.
>
> Я рассерди́лся бо́льше всего́ на то́,
> Что целова́лись не мы́, а го́луби,
> И что прошли́ времена́ Пао́ло и Франче́ски.

The syntactical grouping of the words is the sole factor which distinguishes this rhythmic prose from ordinary prose.

[1] See p. 112.

BIBLIOGRAPHICAL NOTES

Studies in Russian versification are numerous and this list does not claim to be exhaustive. Only the most important works are mentioned. The aim of this selection is to serve as a starting point for further investigation.

BIBLIOGRAPHY

М. П. Штокмар, Библиография работ по стихосложению, М.-Л., 1933. Pp. 184.

> This work, which begins with studies of the sixteenth century, records 1068 items and gives references to reviews. Though annotated, it is not a critical bibliography, and despite the claim of the author, it is not exhaustive. It should be used in conjunction with a review by R. O. Jakobson (*Slavia*, XIII [1934–5], pp. 416–31) and Shtokmar's own supplements (Литературный критик [1936], No. 8, pp. 194–205; No. 9, pp. 235–53).

С. Д. Балухатый, Теория литературы. Аннотированная библиография. I. Общие вопросы. Л., 1929. Pp. 248.

> Questions of versification are dealt with on pp. 164–88 and 220–2. More succinct than Shtokmar's bibliography and concerned only with publications since 1870, this work omits nothing essential and is annotated in a particularly useful manner.

V. M. Žirmunskij, 'Formprobleme in der russischen Literaturwissenschaft', *Zeitschrift für slavische Philologie*, I (1925), pp. 117–52.

> A summary account of the works published between 1914 and 1925. Prosody is treated on pp. 130–8.

Frequent bibliographical data will be found in works listed below.

A great many studies are scattered among the various reviews. But a special effort should be made to consult a periodical which has taken a special interest in questions of Russian prosody: Поэтика. Временник Отдела словесных искусств Гос. Института Истории Искусств (Ленинград). Five numbers appeared between 1926 and 1929, of which the contents are listed on p. 214 of Tomashevsky's Теория литературы.

Reference should be made also to the articles dealing with Russian versification in the Литературная энциклопедия. М., 1930–9.

TERMINOLOGY

The terminology of Russian versification is not yet fixed. On this subject the following dictionary, though it is unsatisfactory, may be consulted:

А. П. Квятковский, Словарь поэтических терминов. М., 1940. Pp. 238.

METRE AND RHYTHM

В. М. Жирмунский, Введение в метрику. Теория стиха (Вопросы поэтики, VI). Л., 1925. Pp. 286.

> This work, containing many, sometimes highly controversial, digressions, nevertheless gives a clear and reasonable introduction to the structure of Russian versification. The notes include a great deal of bibliographical data.

Б. В. Томашевский, Русское стихосложение. Метрика (Вопросы поэтики, II). Петроград, 1923. Pp. 156.

> A more balanced outline than the previous one, but less rich in examples. It includes a study of the stanza, neglected by Zhirmunsky. A bibliography at the end of the volume indicates the principal works on Russian versification.

Б. В. Томашевский, Теория литературы. Поэтика, изд. 5-ое, исправленное. М.-Л., 1930. Pp. 240.

> The section on versification (pp. 71–130) states very briefly essential problems raised by the subject. The bibliography by S. D. Balukhaty which follows the text (pp. 207–33) is a shortened version of his earlier compilation mentioned above.

В. Е. Холшевников, Основы стиховедения: русское стихосложение. Л., 1962. Pp. 151.

> A convenient and reliable outline of Russian versification.

Г. Шенгели, Техника стиха. М., 1960. Pp. 312.

> A helpful introduction into the technique of Russian versification.

Г. Шенгели, Трактат о русском стихе. Часть первая. Органическая метрика, изд. 2-ое, переработанное. М.-П., 1923. Pp. 184.

> The value of this work lies in the numerous frequency-tables for various rhythmic combinations, but not in the author's theoretical arguments.

Л. И. Тимофеев, Проблемы стиховедения. Материалы к социологии стиха. М., 1931. Pp. 232.

> The chapter on syllabic versification is the main attraction of this book. Apart from this, some of the frequency-tables will prove useful.

Л. И. Тимофеев, Очерки теории и истории русского стиха. М., 1958. Pp. 415.

> In the first part some general questions are discussed. In the second part the development of Russian verses is outlined from the beginning to Pushkin inclusive.

К. Тарановски, Руски дводелни ритмови, I–II (Српска Академија Наука, Посебна издања, ccxvii. Одељење литературе и језика, 5). Београд, 1953. Pp. vi+376 and 16 separate frequency-tables.

> This work, written in Serbian, is the best and most comprehensive study on Russian binary metres. It gives a full history of these metres from the time of Trediakovsky to that of Pushkin and his followers.

R. Burgi, A History of the Russian Hexameter. Hamden 17, Connecticut, 1954. Pp. x+208.

> A reliable and well informed study on this particular metre.

C. L. Drage. 'Trochaic Metre in Early Russian Syllabo-Tonic Poetry', The Slavonic and East European Review, xxxviii (1960), pp. 361–79; 'The Rhythmic Development of the Trochaic Tetrameter in Early Russian Syllabo-Tonic Poetry', ibid., xxxix (1961), pp. 346–68.

> Two scholarly articles on the trochaic metre in eighteenth-century poetry.

Б. В. Томашевский, О стихе. Статьи. М.-Л., 1929. Pp. 327.

> A collection of the principal articles by this well-known specialist on Russian verse.

В. В. Томашевский, Стих и язык: филологические очерки. М.-Л., 1959. Pp. 471.

> Another collection of articles. Contains a bibliography of the author's studies of Russian versification.

A. Adamczyk, Grundfragen der russischen Versgeschichte. I. Trediakovskij und die Reform. Breslau, 1940. Pp. 46.

A useful analysis of Trediakovsky's first treatise.

Б. М. Эйхенбаум, Мелодика русского лирического стиха (Сборники по теории поэтического языка). Петроград, 1922. Pp. 199.

An important, but controversial, work on the function of melody in verse. The reader is advised to consult in conjunction with it an article by Zhirmunsky dealing with the same question from another point of view:

В. М. Жирмунский, ,,Мелодика стиха", Мысль, 1922, No. 3, pp. 109–39.

А. Бѣлый, Символизмъ. Сборникъ статей. М., 1910. Pp. 633.

This work is recommended because of one of its articles, Опытъ характеристики русскаго четырехстопнаго ямба (pp. 286–330), which served as a starting point for all subsequent studies of the iambic metres in Russian.

В. М. Жирмунский, Композиция лирических стихотворений (Сборники по теории поэтического языка). Петроград, 1921. Pp. 107.

An important study of the syntactical elements in verse.

Among the special studies concerned with the versification of one particular poet, the following are commended:

Н. В. Лапшина, И. К. Романовский, Б. И. Ярхо, Метрический справочник к стихотворениям Пушкина, М.-Л., 1934. Pp. 144.

An extremely useful work, which, in the form of tables and statistics, gives a complete picture of the structure of Pushkin's verse.

Б. В. Томашевский, ,,Ритмика четырехстопного ямба по наблюдениям над стихом 'Евгения Онегина'", Пушкин и его современники, XXIX–XXX (1918), pp. 144–87. Reprinted in the collection О стихе.

Н. С. Трубецкой, ,,Къ вопросу о стихѣ 'Пѣсенъ Западныхъ Славянъ' Пушкина", Бѣлградскій Пушкинскій Сборникъ (Бѣлградъ, 1937), pp. 31–46.

И. Н. Розанов, ,,Лермонтов в истории русского стиха", Литературное наследство, 43–44 (1941), pp. 425–68.

И. Н. Розанов, Лермонтов — мастер стиха. М., 1942. Pp. 223.

Творчество Маяковского. Сборник статей. М., 1952. Pp. 480.

This collection contains three studies on the structure of Mayakovsky's verse by A. Abramov (pp. 131–62), L. I. Timofeev (pp. 163–209), and M. P. Shtokmar (pp. 258–312), the latter being the least satisfactory of the three.

VERSE RECITATION

С. И. Бернштейн, ,,Звучащая художественная речь и ее изучение", Поэтика, 1 (1926), pp. 41–53.

С. И. Бернштейн, ,,Стих и декламация", Русская речь, новая серия, 1 (1927), pp. 7–41.

L. Gáldi, 'Les variétés de l'accent dans le vers russe', Studia Slavica, vi (1960), pp. 315–29.

RHYME

В. М. Жирмунский, Рифма, ее история и теория (Вопросы поэтики, III). Петроград, 1923. Pp. 337.

The most comprehensive work on rhyme. The bibliography is contained in the notes.

Б. В. Томашевский, ,,К истории русской рифмы", Труды Отдела новой русской литературы, 1 (1948), pp. 233–80.

A short and accurate history of Russian rhyme. Reprinted in the collection Стих и язык.

To complete this study, reference should be made to Rozanov's brief article: И. Н. Розанов, ,,Глагольные рифмы", Ученые Записки Московского Гос. Университета, 127 (1948), pp. 173–8.

Dictionaries of rhyme generally lack special interest. The titles of two of them follow:

Л. Шаховская, Словарь рифмъ русскаго языка. М., 1890. Pp. 339.

Н. Абрамовъ, Полный словарь русскихъ рифмъ („Русскій рифмов-никъ"). Спб., 1912. Pp. 157.

A new dictionary of rhyme is in the course of preparation, by G. V. Bykov. See Доклады и Сообщения Филологического Факультета Московского Гос. Университета, 8 (1948), pp. 67–74.

POPULAR VERSIFICATION

The general works listed above generally take popular versification into account. Beside these, the most advanced work on this subject is:

М. П. Штокмар, Исследования в области русского народного стихосложения. М., 1952. Pp. 422.

> This work is especially valuable for its wealth of examples and its full bibliographical data. A quarter of the book is devoted to existing theories of popular versification in Russia. The author's own arguments, however, cannot be accepted.

R. O. Jakobson, 'Studies in Comparative Slavic Metrics', *Oxford Slavonic Papers*, iii (1952), pp. 21–66.

R. O. Jakobson, 'The Kernel of Comparative Slavic Literature', *Harvard Slavic Studies*, i (1953), pp. 1–81.

> Two interesting, though controversial, studies on the origin of Slavonic popular verse.

H. Peukert, 'Der volkstümliche und literarische russische Vers', Zeitschrift für Slawistik, vi (1961), pp. 606–21.

> A penetrating comparative study of oral and literary Russian verse.

Ф. Е. Коршъ, „О русскомъ народномъ стихосложеніи. I. Былины", Извѣстія отдѣленія русскаго языка и словесности, i (1896), pp. 1–45; ii (1897), pp. 429–500, 501–4. Reprinted in Сборникъ отдѣленія русскаго языка и словесности, lxvii, No. 8 (Спб., 1901). Pp. 121.

N. S. Trubeckoj, 'W sprawie wiersza byliny rosyjskiej', in *Prace ofiarowane Kazimierzowi Wóycickiemu* (Wilno, 1937), pp. 100–10.

Н. С. Трубецкой, „О метрике частушки", Версты, ii (Париж, 1927), pp. 205–23.

INDEX OF POETS

INDEX OF SUBJECT MATTER